VOLLEYBALL

The Game & How to Play It

VOLLEYBALL

The Game & How to Play It

GARY ROSENTHAL

CHARLES SCRIBNER'S SONS
New York

Charles Scribner's Sons
Macmillan Publishing Company
866 Third Avenue, New York, NY 10022
Collier Macmillan Canada, Inc.

Library of Congress Cataloging in Publication Data

Rosenthal, Gary.
  Volleyball, the game and how to play it.

  Includes index.
  1. Volleyball. I. Title.
GV1015.3.R67 1983   796.32'5   82-42661
ISBN 0-684-17908-3

Macmillan books are available at special discounts for bulk purchases for sales promotions, premiums, fund-raising, or educational use. For details, contact:

  Special Sales Director
  Macmillan Publishing Company
  866 Third Avenue
  New York, NY 10022

10 9 8 7 6

Printed in the United States of America

For Louise B. Ketz—
My editor, my friend

ACKNOWLEDGMENTS

Books written as supplements to the acquisition of team sport skills invariably reflect the essential principle of successful team play—the generous giving of each individual to the overall team effort.

I am fortunate in having family, friends, colleagues, and access to organizations, all of whom were eager and willing to give freely of their time, energy, talent, and resources for this project.

To this team I give my sincere thanks for all they contributed, knowing full well that there is no real way to ever show my gratitude. Thanks to:

Bob Rose, my talented and creative friend who uses his camera so well in taking photographs to demonstrate the skills of the sport.

Captain William T. "Buck" Lai of the United States Merchant Marine Academy, for allowing us the privilege of using the outstanding facilities at Kings Point for our photography session.

Coach Thomas Harrigan, volleyball coach for both men and women at the academy, both for making his teams available to us and for contributing his expertise' to photograph skills.

The women's volleyball team at Kings Point: Joan Allatta, Karen Joyce, Beth DeLuc, Kathy Rathberger, Chris Romeika, and Judy Vander Laan.

The men's volleyball team at Kings Point: Willie Barrere, Donald Denig, Brad Fahland, Jeff Kalb, Bill Kraynik, Brian Krenzien, and Alan Raush.

The Spalding Corporation, for providing the photograph on the front of the book jacket.

Gene Nichol, my artistic friend, for his advice and expert drawing of diagrams.

Louise Freeman-Boeg, my English connection, for her special contributions to this project.

Lynne Rosenthal, for providing her skills of organization, typing, and support.

Contents

Introduction

In 1964 volleyball was designated an official team competition of the Olympic Games, held that year in Tokyo. With this new status, volleyball reached the pinnacle of amateur sports, joining such international team sports as basketball and soccer in Olympic competition. Designation as an official Olympic competition is awarded to a sport only after proven recognition that it is participated in by great numbers of players in a majority of nations around the world.

Volleyball is now played in well over one hundred countries and on every continent. Regardless of nationality, ethnic variations, language, geography, and politics, all volleyball is played according to the same set of standardized rules and regulations.

In the United States alone, it is reported that there are more than 65 million participants in organized volley-

1

ball play. How many others are playing recreational or physical education-class volleyball without organized leagues (and, therefore, on a nonreporting basis) is impossible to determine.

On every scholastic level volleyball is part of the physical education curriculum and an integral part of recreation programs. Many junior high and high schools have teams that play in league competitions, culminating in championship tournaments. On the college and university level, league and conference championships are played, and seasons end with national championship tournaments for both men's and women's teams. All of this attests to the fact that volleyball appeals to a widely divergent group of participants that surpasses most other team sports.

To be sure, volleyball's public image was enhanced greatly by its inclusion in the 1964 Summer Olympics. The gold medal-winning Japanese women's team displayed to the world a new, dynamic, and exciting way to play volleyball. The Japanese men's team, while not champions in that initial Olympic year, added new techniques, zest, and excitement to the game with their refined individual and team defensive play. In 1964 the Japanese revolutionized volleyball play as much as their electronic and automobile industries have revolutionized the approach to much of the world's business management.

The Tokyo games were given worldwide exposure through television coverage. The exciting play created a demand for international tours, films, teaching clinics, and more television coverage all over the world. For those people already involved in volleyball, these events were not only seen as rewards and an affirmation of their addiction to the sport, but as proof of the exciting levels of play and variety of styles that were obviously an inherent part of their sport.

Those people who regarded volleyball only as a recreational activity suddenly became aware of the high-powered, dynamic aspect of the sport, which in turn fostered a new approach to the game. School coaches and teachers began upgrading their own knowledge of the game and revitalized their programs on all levels. Volleyball had suddenly been given more serious recognition, study, and application to sports programs, not only in America, but throughout the world.

In 1895, almost seventy years before its designation as an Olympic sport, volleyball was devised by William G. Morgan, director of physical education at the Holyoke, Massachusetts, YMCA. Morgan's aim was to provide an activity for generally sedentary middle-aged businessmen that could be played indoors in inclement weather, offer healthy but not too strenuous exercise, and, at the same time, provide enough fun to keep the participants coming back for more. The YMCA has branches all over the United States as well as in many foreign countries. Aside from the other amenities the Y offers, physical activity has always been a foundation of its philosophy. This philosophy proved to be the catalyst that popularized volleyball throughout the world.

As an interesting sidelight, just four years earlier, in 1891, Dr. James Naismith, also affiliated with the YMCA, designed a game for the very same reasons. He hung peach baskets at either end of the gym and created the game of basketball.

Rather than hanging peach baskets at either end of the gym, Morgan strung a tennis net across the gym at a height of 6 feet 6 inches from the floor. The newly devised heavy leather basketball, while well suited for passing and dribbling, was simply too tough on the fingers for volleying, so Morgan decided to use the rubber bladder inside the basketball for play.

As Morgan had hoped, the game was fun and brought just the right amount of activity to its participants. The old boys had their workout without the knocks, bruises, and strains of the other sports of the day.

Morgan held introductory and teaching clinics in volleyball for other Y physical directors in the area, and the game spread throughout the Y network with great fervor, so much so that volleyball's early history, growth, and spread is enmeshed almost totally with the YMCA and its far-reaching organization. Others tried the new sport and received the same enthusiastic response.

Morgan's original game was quite different from today's game. The original playing area was 25 feet by 50 feet, as opposed to the present-day size of 29 feet 6 inches by 59 feet. The net was originally 6 feet 6 inches from the floor, but is now 7 feet 11⅝ inches off the floor for men and 7 feet 4⅛ inches for women. Any number of players were allowed to play and the number of hits on each side of the net were unlimited. If the first serve didn't make it over the net, a second serve was taken. All in all, the game was designed for large groups, which, of course, resulted in a good time for all.

As is the case in so many recreational activities that originate strictly as fun and leisure-time pursuits, the inherent possibilities of volleyball as a competitive sport soon became apparent to many of its devotees. As players developed skills and team tactics, a natural evaluation began to take place. Players wanted more playing time, contact with the ball, participation in the flow of the game, and physically strenuous competition.

From the basic and crowded-court game of Morgan's time evolved the high-powered, fast-paced game of today. To meet the demands of players, the game was improved by raising the net, reducing the number of players on a side to six, adding rotation to allow everyone on the court a more varied role, giving everyone a chance to serve, reducing control of the ball with the hands, adding blocking, and refining individual techniques.

All sports, volleyball included, change for the better as players become more skilled, because skilled players are able to operate within more complex team strategies. As team strategies become more sophisticated and more consistent, individual skills are refined to perfect countermeasures for newly evolving strategies. From this evolutionary process comes the never-ending changes, adaptations, and developments that make sports more dynamic.

Volleyball had only one serious handicap to overcome in its early development. Its original purpose—to provide a not-too-strenuous game for middle-aged businessmen—combined with the fact that it was played at a leisurely pace on crowded courts in school, gave it an image of being a slow, dull game. But the eventual modification and evolution of the rules by players who knew better, revitalized the game and spread its appeal around the world, culminating in Oylmpic designation.

Today, volleyball is recognized as a competitive sport that requires agility, quick movement, coordination, physical conditioning, and determination. Tactics are complex and the levels of individual skill needed to carry out these tactics have increased. The pace of the action in competitive volleyball demands levels of physical conditioning equal to the demands of any other team sport. Players have to be in top shape for the fast, demanding, coordinated, and relatively uninterrupted pace of the game, and the training and conditioning needed to play volleyball can lead to overall endurance, strength, and physical well-being.

Volleyball also presents a challenge in coordination. Many individual skills must be coordinated with others in order to play at a high level. The vertical jump must be coordinated with the hit to execute the spike. The dive or roll on the floor must be coordinated to execute the dig for a purposeful pass. No skill or technique stands on its own—all are the result of coordinated movements and specific skilled applications.

However, one of the inherent appeals of volleyball is that the game can be played at virtually any skill level with joy and exuberance, well before one masters the higher level power volleyball skills. So, let it be consolation to the beginning player, regardless of age or sex, to know that coordination, timing, skill execution, and complicated tactics will come with experience and diligent practice.

It is also important to note that volleyball is truly a game for everyone. It can be played by girls and boys and men and women on levels commensurate with their age, skills, physical condition, and interest. While size in terms of height can be a decided advantage, there is more of a demand for talented players than for tall players. In general, size counts much less than skill and physical conditioning, making the game particularly rewarding for younger players looking for a highly competitive sport.

Volleyball also develops a good sense of team play and cooperation. The constant flow from offense to defense and the need for each player to be ready at all times contribute to the camaraderie of team play. It doesn't take long for players to learn that this is a sport that is absolutely dependent on teamwork.

Aside from fielding varsity teams for both sexes, schools encourage volleyball because it provides for safe, large group participation, both indoors and out, all year round. Groups of eighteen or even more can play, and with intelligent planning, as many as fifty students can be accommodated for practice and skill drills with little problem. Of further appeal to schools is the relatively inexpensive costs involved. Gym uniforms are worn since players on opposing teams are kept apart by the net rather than color of jersey.

The most costly items in the volleyball program are the ball and the net and its supporting standards. Volleyballs range from inexpensive but utilitarian rubber and plastic models to the more expensive leather balls. Standards and nets are an investment that will last for years with proper care and storage.

What has been written to this point about volleyball's broad, participatory appeal could be applied to other sports by their proponents. But, there is one aspect of the game that gives volleyball its uniqueness. It can be played and enjoyed from its Olympic level down to the simpler variations of the game, which while simpler, still provide the recreation sought by its participants. There is also no need for elaborate playing areas or costly installations. In fact, more volleyball is participated in on a recreational basis than in formal, structured programs. It is hard to find an adult of either sex who has not participated in recreational volleyball.

The recreational aspect of volleyball is nothing new. As far back as 1918, during World War I, volleyballs were sent to American soldiers in Europe, as they were in World War II. When nets weren't available, a length of rope was stretched between two trees or other similar supports. Being able to set up a volleyball court so simply has carried over into everyday recreational play. While a net is preferred, a rope will suffice, and a volleyball and two tall-enough sticks complete the equipment list for recreational play.

Beaches, parks, backyards, open fields, schoolyards, swimming pools, and even streets in Brooklyn, have all been used as volleyball courts. Once the net or rope is put up, the rest is easy. Boundary lines take the form of lines dug in the sand; towels, jackets, or shirts placed in corners; chalk lines drawn on compatible surfaces; or the edge of the swimming pool. Local rules prevail, predicated on the basic rules and regulations of volleyball, such as no more than three hits on one side of the net, rotation, and so on.

Teams can be made up of any number of players and mixed in terms of sex, age, skill, or anything that particularly appeals to the group playing. *Sports Illustrated* magaine recently ran a story on two-player volleyball that is played on the beaches of California. Such recreational games very often contain the ferocity of more organized games, again attesting to the fact that volleyball can reach whatever heights its participants want.

Most recreational volleyball is played by large groups at a picnic or a day at the beach. In virtually all of these games, the basic rules of volleyball are adhered to, and the players approach the game with a combination of seriousness and fun. Recreational volleyball provides all the things that a leisure-time physical activity should provide—enjoyment, a good workout, friendly competition, and social interaction.

The universality of volleyball lies in its easy adaptability to the needs and skill and physical conditioning levels of its participants, such as lowering the net, reducing the size of the playing area, relaxing the rules by mutual consent, or modifying the rules to allow for different mixes of players. It is obvious that volleyball's easy adaptability to the specific needs of people makes it the most widely played game in the world.

Volleyball Variations

NEWCOMB

Newcomb is the classic volleyball lead-up or introductory game. It has all the elements of regulation volleyball except the volleying of the ball. The game is played by throwing the volleyball back and forth over the net. Newcomb is used as an introduction to volleyball rules and concepts and is taught in the fourth or fifth grades. With some changes, Newcomb can be more sophisticated and more fun, but first let's look at the basic game.

Two teams of from six to nine players each line up on opposite sides of the net. To start the match, the ball is thrown over the net from the right rear end line. The player catching the ball then throws the ball back over the net from the spot where it was caught. A point is earned when a player on the catching side fails to catch a thrown ball that lands within the playing area or if the ball is touched and dropped. If the ball is thrown out-of-bounds, the other team scores a point. The number of points needed to win the game is usually fifteen, but teams can play for any number of points.

A variation of Newcomb that can be enjoyed by enthusiastic but less talented adults is played the same way. The variation is to allow three passes to be made on the same side of the net before returning the ball over the net. Through rapid, accurate passing the ball direction can be changed to outmaneuver the opponents. If the ball is dropped during the passing process, the point is lost. This variation can lead to hilarity and excitement as the ball is passed faster and faster and all players are forced to respond to the actions of the passed ball. A good workout will be had by all.

MORE THAN SIX ON A SIDE

Six on a side is the regulation for competitive volleyball in the scholastic, collegiate, national, and international games for both men and women. Given the 30 foot by 30 foot size of half the court, six on a side provides the right balance of space to be covered by the players. Once there are more than six on a side, the space per player is reduced and each player has less to do. Games played by more than six on a side tend to be more recreational than competitive and are generally played more for their social aspects than for the values ascribed to competitive six-on-a-side volleyball.

There is nothing wrong with playing volleyball with up to ten players on a side as long as it is understood that these games should be played for fun. Ten or even twelve players per side has its place socially and even in physical education classes where space may be at a premium. More than six on a side is not helpful when practicing or training for competition. The crowded court does not lend itself to improving individual or team tactics. On the other hand, games played with fewer than six players will certainly improve skills and techniques, and will go a long way toward developing physical condition.

FOUR-PLAYER VOLLEYBALL

Four-player volleyball serves many basic purposes. It provides greater action and greater demands on players by forcing them to range farther and faster over the court.

The rules of four-player volleyball are the same as six player with one exception—backcourt players may come to the net to spike or block the ball.

General offense tactics provide for a designated setter in the middle and a spiker at either side of the net to maintain the rhythm of the desired pass, set, or spike.

When defending, the general tactic is to try to have two players block at the net. The player at the net who is not involved with the two-man block should retreat quickly from the net to assist the backcourt player. In this way both players in the backcourt are ready to dig after a spike, pass a dink shot, or go after a deflected block.

Four-player rotation is done in a clockwise direction prior to serving, just as it is done in the six-player game.

With more of a court area for each player to cover, four-player volleyball has other values besides good, strenuous competition. Used in practice situations, players can sharpen their skills, anticipate plays, and, in general, develop court sense. It also contributes to the conditioning program by forcing players to range far and wide and to recover quickly, keeping in the game at all times.

DOUBLES VOLLEYBALL

Here is a variation of volleyball devised mainly for the well-conditioned, skilled, and most dedicated players. The rules of play are generally the same as they are in six on a side. It is easy to imagine the speed, anticipatory skill, individual techniques, and team play necessary just to keep the ball in play. After all, two players are covering an area more frequently patrolled by six.

To reduce the pressure on the players somewhat, the number of points needed to win is reduced from fifteen to eleven. Sometimes the court is shortened by 5 feet on each side, thus reducing the area to be covered. But even with the reduction of court size and the number of points needed to win, the game is strenuous, demanding all of the skills and court sense possible.

Naturally, the tactics for doubles is far different from the normal game. The desired sequence of play is the familiar pass-set-spike pattern. The player receiving the serve must pass the ball to his partner, who sets the ball for the original receiver, who has now run up to the net to become a spiker and spike the ball.

In doubles play, the serve takes on greater importance. Power is not as important as is accurate placement. The objective of the serve—as always, but even more critical in doubles—is to serve the ball accurately to spots on the court that will preclude the establishment of the pass-set-spike sequence. Deep serves can interrupt the sequence as can serves that draw the receiver far to his right or left.

On defense, both players must play back for effective coverage, the idea being to play the ball in front of you. Therefore, blocking is virtually nonexistent in doubles.

Doubles can also be a valuable tool for developing individual skills, court sense, anticipation, and physical conditioning. Better players can use doubles as pressure drills during and after practice and in the off-season to maintain fitness and skill levels.

MIXED VOLLEYBALL

One of the most delightful aspects of volleyball is how easily it lends itself to the mix of men and women, boys and girls. Only a game that is predicated on skill, quick movement, team play, and physical condition, and not strength or power, can involve both sexes. Mixed volleyball teams and competition are extremely popular, and men and women and boys and girls can play alongside one another against teams of similar composition.

Mixed volleyball is played with from two to six players on a side. The regulation net height is 8 feet and all other rules of volleyball apply except one—if the ball is played more than once on your side of the court, one of the touches must be made by a female player. Obviously, this rule was added to prevent unnecessary male domination of the play.

Further, positions on the court and serving order must alternate—male, female, male, female, and so on. With an odd number of players, two players of the same sex, because of mathematical necessity, will serve consecutively.

The demonstrated skill and aggressive play of women and girls post no liabilities to the quality of play in mixed volleyball. Female passing, digging, and general offensive and defensive play is at levels equal to most male levels. The only problem females may encounter is in spiking and blocking, because the net is set at 8 feet, nearly 8 inches above the height called for in women's play. But team tactics and smart play can help alleviate this problem.

BEACH VOLLEYBALL

Beaches and volleyball are made for one another. The combination of sun, sand, fresh air, open space, social dynamics, and the love of competition all blend together to make beach volleyball a happening. On beaches from Long Island to California, in Tel Aviv and on the Riviera, beach volleyball is played and enjoyed by millions. Whether it be a friendly, social match or an intense, highly competitive game, beach volleyball is a fantastic way to compete, get a good workout, and meet people, all while getting a nice, even suntan.

Playing on a beach modifies the game greatly. Wind and sun, always a factor in outdoor games, are challenges that particularly influence play. With the wind coming from behind, serves, passes, and high sets will be affected. Playing into the wind takes extra power in the serves and in getting the ball up to the net. Cross winds can cause the ball to float, veer, or drop, forcing the player to dive and dig for the ball. For beach volleyball players, these elemental forces add more spice to the game, making it that much more exciting. To compensate for these humanly uncontrollable factors, most beach volleyball rules call for changing court sides after every five points, thereby balancing out any prolonged disadvantages.

Playing on sand further changes the game. The fact that sand is not stable means that more drive has to be put into leg movements, including getting height for spiking and blocking. While these problems relating to play on sand may seem to be drawbacks, there is also a plus factor that contributes to the game. It has been known for a long time that running and training on sand does wonders for strengthening and developing leg muscles. So, general conditioning benefits result from playing on sand.

One of the most exciting aspects of playing on sand is being able to dive and roll to get to the ball without fear of injury. Some of the most spectacular plays in defensive volleyball are performed on sand.

The rules of volleyball are generally the same on sand as when the game is played in the gymnasium. There are, however, some rules designed to compensate for the less stable surface. The net is set at 7 feet 8½ inches on loose-packed sand and at 7 feet 10 inches on hard-packed sand. Another change in the rules is that on the soft sand surface a player is allowed to step across the center line, provided that player does not interfere with an opponent.

Mixed volleyball, for obvious reasons, is extremely popular on the beaches of the world. Six, four, and even three on a side are played universally. But, the most popular of the strenuous volleyball games is the demanding game of beach doubles. While not yet an Olympic sport, beach doubles volleyball reached its high point when it was featured in the August 23, 1982, issue of *Sports Illustrated.*

While the basic rules of volleyball still prevail, beach doubles has some of its own special rules. The server may serve from any place behind the baseline. The server is not restricted to the right third of the baseline. Blockers may not reach over the net, which is permitted in regulation six-man volleyball. Two time-outs, each one minute long are permitted and, I might add, needed. The intensity and ferocity of doubles played on a beach is only matched by the spectacular plays that inevitably are part of the game.

Volleyball, in all its forms and variations, when played on equitable, competitive levels, is truly an exciting, demanding, and fulfilling sport. Its future growth and development is guaranteed not simply by its long-in-coming recognition, but in its fundamental appeal to participants in terms of skill, teamwork, adaptability, and wholesome, joyful recreational and competitive need ful-fillment.

The Serve

The serve in volleyball is surrounded by a rather different set of circumstances from those usually present in most other sports. Certainly, all sports have their own method of putting the ball into play, but volleyball is different for the following reasons: a team can only score points while serving, and each player on the team must rotate into the serving position and serve. Because of these rather unique circumstances, it is obvious that each player must learn to serve well.

Serving well means that each player must serve with the objective of scoring a point. The serve should never be used to put the ball into play. Skilled serving techniques add immeasurably to attacking, offensive volleyball.

Only the server knows where he or she will be directing the ball, with how much force or velocity, and with what sort of spin or effect. With good service techniques and practice, all players will be able to achieve speed and controlled and accurate placement, and impart floats, wobbles, or English (spin) to the ball. All of these add considerably to the pressures put on the receiving player.

SERVING RULES

The service area is situated in both right rear corners of the volleyball court at both end lines. The service area is 9 feet 10 inches wide and should extend back 6 feet. Servers may stand as far behind the end line as they wish within the service area. The server may not touch any of the court lines or step outside of the marked service area until he or she has made contact with the ball. It is not against the rules for the server's arm or body to extend over any of the court lines that define the service area prior to contacting the ball.

The server may use an open hand, the fist, or an arm to propel the ball over the net into the opponent's side of the court. The ball must not touch any player on the serving team before going over the net nor can it touch the net or the antennas.

SERVING ROTATION

Serving rotation begins with the right back player being the opening server. This same player continues serving until the serving team loses the point or the game is completed.

When the service is lost, the ball is turned over to the opposing team, which begins its service rotation with its right back player. When possession of the ball is regained, all players rotate positions one place, with the player in the right front position moving to the right back position, always becoming the next server. (See Diagram 1.)

THE UNDERHAND SERVE

The underhand serve is the simplest serve. It is the easiest to learn, the easiest to control, and the easiest to quickly put into game situations. Beginning volleyball players of both sexes, of all ages, and of different degrees of fitness, strength, and coordination will find the underhand serve readily attainable.

Its real value lies in the fact that its basic simplicity makes it a reliable and consistent method of getting the ball over the net and into play. This factor is particularly important in sustaining both interest and play in teaching and recreational volleyball sessions.

The underhand serve does not, by its very nature, have the effect of the more devastating overhand serve because of its higher trajectory. But, for beginners or just for fun, the underhand serve gets the job done. When the basic techniques have been mastered, variations can be added to put some surprises into this seemingly guile-free serve.

Technique

The server stands facing the net, with the left foot forward and both knees comfortably flexed. The ball rests in the palm of the left hand, and the left arm is extended across the front of the body. This position puts the ball just

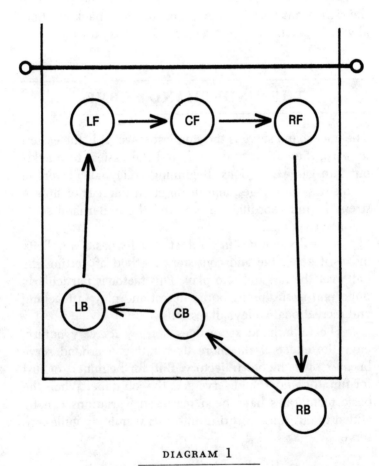

DIAGRAM 1

Serving Rotation. The right back (RB) player is always the server.

slightly higher than the left knee and in line vertically with the head. This starting position provides the platform from which the ball will be struck by the right hand. The starting position is reversed for left-handed servers.

When ready to serve, the right arm (or striking arm) is swung straight back and then forward in a pendulum-type motion to make contact with the ball. Contact with the ball is made just below its horizontal midline with the heel and knuckles of the hand if the hand is closed, or with just the heel of the hand if the hand is open. Regardless of which striking surface of the hand is preferred, the wrist must be locked and held rigid at the time of contact with the ball.

The head and neck should be bent forward and the eyes should be focused on the ball through the swing, contact, and into the follow-through. Jerking the head up too quickly to watch the ball's flight will cause the body to straighten up, thus lifting the ball too high.

Adding controlled power to the ball is accomplished by transferring your body weight to the arm swing. In the ready-to-serve position, transfer the body's weight to the rear foot. As the striking arm is brought forward, transfer the weight smoothly from the rear foot to the forward foot. The principle is the same as that of a baseball pitcher, who transfers his weight from back leg to front leg. The power for the serve results from the forward movement of the body and combines with the swing of the arm.

The follow-through is directed straight through the ball in the direction of the intended line of flight. It is extremely important that the swing of the arm, the contact with the ball, and the follow-through be in line with the intended flight. Any variation in the sequence will alter the ball's flight path.

As promised, there are ways of adding some spice to the basic underhand serve. Once a player can put the ball

PHOTO 1. *The Underhand Serve. Server faces the net with the left foot forward, the ball resting in the palm of the left hand and the left arm extended across the front of the body.*

over the net consistently and with a fair degree of control and accuracy, he or she can purposely alter the ball's flight pattern through variations of the basic contact and striking pattern.

In striking the ball on the vertical midline just below the horizontal midline, we are able to achieve the right amount of lift to clear the net and at the same time have the ball follow a straight path. Repetitive practice gives the server the ability to put the ball over the net consistently, *but* it also has made the basic serve so predictable

PHOTO 2. *The right arm is swung back and then forward, with the eyes focused on the ball through the swing.*

PHOTO 3. *The follow-through is directed straight through the ball in the intended line of flight.*

that opponents can watch the server and anticipate where the serve is being directed. This negates the purpose of the serve because it allows the opponent time to set up for the return. Predictability must be removed from the service.

Variety, which results in unpredictability, can be accomplished by contacting the ball slightly to the left or right of the vertical midline but still just below the horizontal midline. Striking the ball crisply to the right of the vertical midline will cause the ball to travel to the server's left or crosscourt on the opponent's side of the net. Similarly, striking the ball just to the left of the vertical midline will make the ball travel to the server's right, bending into the left side of the opponent's court. In both instances, the starting position is the same. The variation comes at the point of contact. The opponent will not be able to predict direction if the server observes the same basic technique of the serve.

Another option available to the underhand server is the "floater" serve. The floating serve actually goes through the air following no prescribed pattern, moving left or right apparently at its own whim. Here's why.

In previously described serves, brisk contact with the ball combined with follow-through puts spin on the ball. This spin, when meeting the resistance of the air, causes the ball to move in the direction opposite the contact point.

To achieve the floating effect, spin has to be taken off the ball. This is accomplished by striking the ball just below the horizontal midline but without any follow-through. When the player's hand makes contact with the ball, it should stop. Striking the ball in this way imparts very little spin to the ball, and with no spin helping it along, the ball cannot "cut" through the air—it actually has to fight its way through its flight. In traveling with no spin, the ball is affected by any air currents hitting it, imbalances in the ball itself, which can cause compression

DIAGRAM 2

To achieve lift and straight direction, the ball is contacted on the vertical midline just below the horizontal midline.

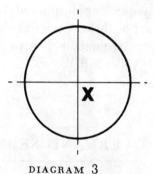

DIAGRAM 3

Striking the ball to the right of the vertical midline causes the ball to travel to the server's left or crosscourt.

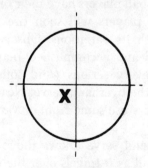

DIAGRAM 4

Striking the ball to the left of the vertical midline causes the ball to travel to the server's right.

variations at contact, or by the positioning of the valve system built into the ball to fill it. Any of these will cause a nonspinning ball to unpredictably float left and right, rise, drop and generally act peculiar. This erratic flight adds greatly to an opponent's problem of setting up for a serve return.

The underhand serve is easy to learn and easy to put into game situations. With practice it can be altered to provide greater attacking capabilities. It should be used as a fundamental skill in preparing for more advanced serving skills. Its greatest benefit lies in the fact that it brings relatively quick application and satisfaction to beginning players. For these reasons the underhand serve is still the most popular method of serving among beginning and recreational volleyball players.

OVERHAND SERVE

Just as baseball pitchers have their fastballs, soccer players their powerful instep kicks, and boxers their knockout punches, volleyball players have their big serve. Motivated and aggressive players will soon tire of the underhand serve, even with its variations. Observers of volleyball's more advanced and accomplished players will soon see that virtually every serious (and some not as serious) player utilizes the overhand serve. Nearly all competitive volleyball players use some from or variation of the overhand serve.

The overhand serve allows the player to put more speed on the ball as it travels over the net and provides a shorter trajectory. The shorter trajectory is attained because the ball is contacted far higher from the floor than in the underhand serve. The acquisition of speed and a shorter, floater trajectory gives the opponent less time to prepare for receiving service—an easily recognizable advantage to the serving team.

The power and speed made possible through overhand serving is generated by getting the weight of the body, or as much as possible, behind the arm and the contact hand. The flat trajectory is accomplished by striking the ball high, at the top of the reach of the extended arm and hand.

The point of contact with the ball, as well as the method of getting to the point of contact, is similar to the overhand serve of tennis or the whiplike overhand throw used by baseball outfielders. What is consistent to these three examples is the fact that the weight of the body is applied to the lever—in these cases, the arm—just prior to contact, and in so doing, adds velocity and force to the contact.

To achieve this chain of action, timing becomes crucial and basic understanding of technique becomes important. Also important is the knowledge that individual differences always operate in performing skills. Once the player grasps the principles that go into the serve, the following description can be adapted to meet his or her personal needs.

Technique

The starting position for the overhand serve is taken with the server standing from 2 to 5 feet behind the service line. It is important that the player not be too close to the line since it is possible that the server's forward motion could bring him into contact with the service area line causing a foul.

PHOTO **4.** *The Overhand Serve. The player should face the court with the left foot placed ahead of the right. The lifting arm and hand hold the ball around shoulder level, with the striking hand on top of the ball.*

PHOTO 5. *The lift should put the ball approximately 3 feet into the air, at which point the weight should shift to the front leg.*

PHOTO 6. *As the weight comes forward, the fully cocked and extended arm swings forward to make contact with the ball.*

PHOTO 7. *The follow-through is directed straight through the ball in the intended line of flight.*

The player should face the court at an angle that is both comfortable and compatible with individual preferences, which are developed and determined in practice. For right-handed servers, the left foot should be placed ahead of the right approximately shoulder width apart. The knees should be slightly flexed with more weight on the rear foot than on the front.

Just as in tennis, the toss of the ball and the transfer of body weight depend on good timing. It is at this point, immediately prior to the act of serving, that concentration begins. The server's eyes are on the ball and must remain on the ball from start, through the lift, through the forward motion and swing and into contact.

When ready to serve, most of the body's weight should shift to the rear foot. When the transfer has been made, the ball is ready to be lifted into striking position. Please note that *toss* is the word most frequently used in volleyball terminology, but *toss* implies a certain carelessness that does not belong in the sequence for serving. Actually, the thrust of the body and arm under the ball lift it into the air to serving height. Concentrate on *lift* and the process of attaining lift and the feeling will come to you.

The lifting arm and hand hold the ball comfortably around shoulder level. The striking hand is on top of the ball, steadying and adding to better control. The lifting of the ball begins with a simultaneous short flex of the rear leg and the upward extension of the lifting arm. The contact feels natural. The point of withdrawal for the contact arm will occur when the hand is in the general area of the neck and ear.

The lift should put the ball approximately 3 feet into the air, above and just in front of the right shoulder. When the ball reaches the highest point of the lift, the weight transfer from the rear leg to the front leg begins. As the weight comes forward, the fully cocked and extended arm swings forward to make contact with the ball. Contact should be made with the heel of the open hand since this surface provides a relatively flat, hard striking area. The wrist is locked and held rigid at contact.

The follow-through to the overhand serve reflects the variety of possibilities that may be applied to the ball's flight. Most overhand servers employ the "floater" serve. The same striking technique that applies to the underhand serve to achieve float applies to the overhand serve. Contact with the ball must be made at the intersection of the vertical midline and the horizontal midline or just slightly below it. Contact must be crisp and of short duration or else spin will be imparted to the ball. There is no follow-through. The arm must be deliberately stopped at contact. This technique of stopping the follow-through at contact will result in a spin-free serve and the desired erratic flight over the net.

For the beginner who wants spin on the ball, all the techniques of the overhand serve remain the same. The spin, right or left, is attained by contacting the ball on or just slightly to the left or right of the vertical midline at the horizontal midline. The full follow-through—down, forward, and across the server's body—will keep the hand in contact with the ball for a much longer period of time. This results in spin.

SERVING DRILLS

It is important to practice the basic serves, until control and consistency are acquired. When the server has reached the point of controlled, consistent serving, he or she will be ready for more advanced serving techniques described in a later chapter.

There are two important factors of a volleyball match that must be taken into account when designing serving drills: (1) every player on the team must take a turn at serving, and (2) each player is expected to serve well throughout the match, from start to finish. The implications of these two factors are obvious. Every member of the team must practice serving with regularity and intensity at every practice session. There are no serving specialists or "designated" servers. Every team member must become a service specialist with controlled and accurate serves as the objective.

The second point also makes it clear that serving practice should come at the start, midpoint, and end of practice. By practicing at these different time periods, players are best able to approximate the fatigue levels that will occur in the course of play. At the start of the game, each player has to deal primarily with the tension that builds as the player approaches serving for the first time. Toward the middle of the match, tensions are gone, the player should be thoroughly warmed up, and serving should be good at this point. It is here, however, depending on the intensity of play, that the fatigue level begins to increase. Players must now apply greater concentration to the serve. In the later stages of a hard-played match, tiredness and exhaustion begin to take their toll on the individual player. Here is where concentration, physical conditioning, and coordination are stretched to their limits.

For these reasons, the serve must be practiced and drilled at various times throughout the practice session. Each player should serve at least 75 times at each practice. Always keep in mind when practicing serves that the serve can be the most effective scoring weapon in the team's offensive arsenal.

Drill #1. All available courts should be free of receivers. Players should be divided along the end lines of the courts so that they can serve back and forth over the net. Each pair of players should have a ball so that plenty of serving practice can be had by all. The players take turns, as the ball comes to them, fielding the ball, getting set, and serving the ball across the net. By having all players behind the end lines, the server can see where the ball landed on the other side of the net. The server should always move into the service box unless he or she is working on practicing serving down the line or straight serves. In those cases, direction is the purpose and that can be practiced from anywhere along the back line. (See Diagram 5.)

Drill #2. Set up a full team on the receiving side against a server. This is a good drill for practicing service variations by working on different spins, floats, and speeds, as well as practicing controlled directionality. The receiving team practices handling serves and can actually go through a pass-set-spike flow with no defense against it. (See Diagram 6.)

Drill #3. To add some interest to service practice, objects such as traffic cones, chairs, or towels should be placed on the receiving side. Points can be awarded each player for each object hit, with the coach calling out, prior to the serve, the object to be hit. In using targets, players sometimes have the tendency to take pace off the serve for the sake of accuracy. It is important that the coach discourage any

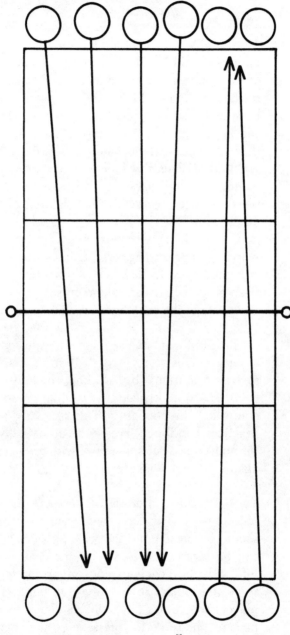

DIAGRAM 5

Serving Drill #1 is a full-team drill with all players participating on all available courts. Players are divided along the end lines of the courts and serve back and forth over the net.

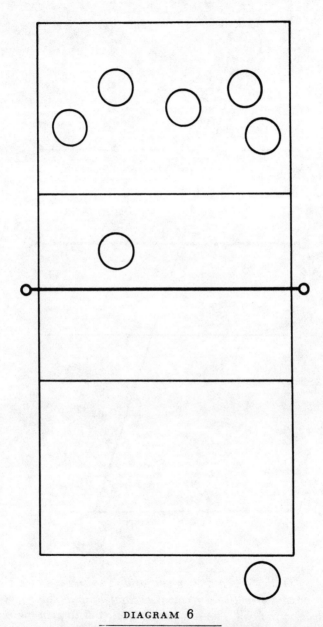

DIAGRAM 6

Serving Drill #2. Players take turns at serving into a receiving team. The server's objective is to serve to vulnerable areas. The receiving team's objective is to pass to the setter and then spike, as in a game situation.

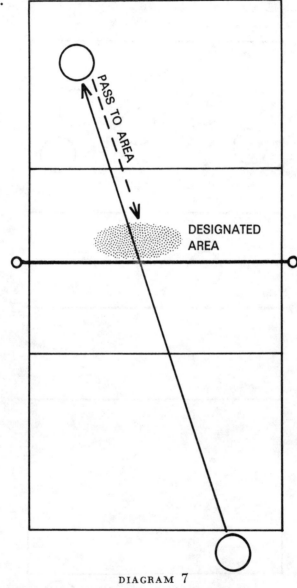

DIAGRAM 7

Serving Drill #4 is a one-on-one drill. The server's objective is to serve the ball to a receiver accurately with spin, speed, or float on the ball. The receiver's objective is to play the ball cleanly to a designated area.

easing up and insist that the players serve with the same pace and intensity used in a match.

Drill #4. Competition can be added to service practice by having two players—a server and a receiver —play against each other. The receiver is given an area to pass to that approximates the place where the setter would line up. The server serves to the receiver and gets one point each time the receiver misplays the ball or fails to pass to the designated area. The receiver gets one point each time the serve is handled well, that is, passed to the designated area.

The variations for serving practice are many. Always a factor is the individual weaknesses of players that must then be worked on through individual instruction. Service drills, especially with beginners, must be designed to give lots of actual practice to develop consistency, variety, control, and confidence.

Passing and Setting

Once the volleyball has been served, all play that follows, until one team or the other loses the point, is called passing. Passing begins with the reception of the serve and the subsequent controlled hitting of the ball from one player to another and culminates in putting the ball over the net into the opponent's court. The opponent then uses passing to set up the return over the net.

Because the rules of volleyball clearly state that a player may not catch or carry the ball, various passing techniques have evolved that allow the player to volley the ball in a controlled manner. While all of these techniques are covered under the general heading of passing, more specific names have been given to different passes in an effort to descriptively simplify discussion, teaching, and application of these skills. The terminology that follows is consistent with terminology used wherever volleyball is played.

THE OVERHAND PASS

The overhand pass made its appearance in the early days of volleyball. It was originally used to receive serves, pass the ball to a teammate, or set up another player at the net for a spike. With the coming of faster and more powerful serves, use of the overhand pass to receive hard serves or spikes proved impractical. Players were simply unable to get into a position quickly enough to receive the ball with both hands simultaneously in accordance with the rules.

However, the beginning player is not faced with smashing serves or downward driving spikes. Rather, he or she deals mainly with the higher trajectory serves and the softer, beginner's version of the spike. It is therefore important that beginning players learn the basic overhand pass so that serves can be handled cleanly and in a controlled manner and so that the ball can be passed to a teammate and then on over the net.

Another point that must be emphasized is that the basic overhand pass has evolved in "the set." The set is a more advanced version of the overhand pass that was designed and is regularly used, as its name implies, to accurately set up or place the ball in the air in position for another player to spike it. Learning the overhand pass is basic to progressing to more advanced volleyball skills.

Basic to the execution of the overhead pass is getting into position under the ball. Whether the ball is above the head or at waist level, the player must adjust to the height by bending the knees, even if the bend results in a deep squatting position. Being in a balanced, ready position under the ball is of paramount importance to successful passing.

Having reached the position under the ball, the head should be up with the eyes focused on the incoming ball.

PHOTO 8. *The Overhead Pass. A balanced, ready position under the ball is very important in successful passing. The head should be up, with the eyes focused on the ball.*

PHOTO 9. *The Overhead Pass. Having reached the position under the ball, the elbows are out to the side at shoulder level, and the hands are up with the fingers spread.*

PHOTO 10. *Ready Position for Passing. In the proper ready position, the hands will be about 2 inches apart and the index fingers about 3 to 4 inches apart.*

PHOTO 11. *The Pass. As contact is made, the player extends the whole body in the direction of the intended pass.*

The elbows are out to the side at about shoulder level, the hands are up with the fingers spread. One foot is slightly ahead of the other with the knees comfortably bent to maintain balance and to provide a solid base for contact.

The ball is contacted by the fingers and thumbs only —never the palms of the hands. To be sure to keep the palms off the ball, cup the fingers and thumbs. This puts some space between the fingers and palm on contact. Both hands must contact the ball simultaneously. To achieve the correct striking plane, both wrists must be flexed back as far as they can go so that the palms face upward in the direction of the incoming ball.

In the proper ready position, the hands will be about 2 inches apart and the index fingers about 3 to 4 inches apart. The player is able to watch the incoming ball framed by the natural "viewfinder" framed by the thumbs and index fingers.

As contact is made, the player extends the whole body in the direction of the intended pass. The knees, hips, upper body, arms, elbows, wrists, and fingers drive up into the ball from underneath. With practice this upward drive-train effect through the ball can be modified and controlled. The player, through practice, will soon learn how much upward body thrust is needed to place the ball where he or she wants it.

THE FOREARM PASS

The forearm pass also goes by the name of the "bump pass." The original name, forearm pass, is simply derived from the fact that the ball is played underhand off the forearms.

In the early days of the game, the forearm pass was employed by players who had difficulty in returning serves. Player difficulties included not being able to get into good position for an overhand pass because of the fast approach of the ball, getting to the ball too late in its flight, or playing the ball poorly with open palms in the underhand position, resulting in a foul and loss of the point.

It soon became apparent that this forearm technique for poorer players could be adapted, modified, and, with proper application, become a valuable passing technique. After all, if the forearm pass could be used to handle low difficult serves, it could also be used to handle any low ball or any downward driving ball resulting from a power serve or spike. Skillful use of the forearm pass made obvious its use for playing balls extremely close to the floor. Going for these low balls became known as "digging the ball out," giving rise to the term "dig." (More on the technique and application of the "dig" in the advanced skills section.)

Before we look at the techniques used in the forearm pass, it is important to understand the components that go into it. The forearms are used to allow us to get under the ball, particularly in the case of balls dropping rapidly below the waist. The rules state that only one simultaneous contact of the hands or arms may be used by a player. This means that both forearms must contact the ball at the same time. Further, in order to contact the ball on the forearms, the broadest and flattest areas must make contact with the ball.

Also, the contact made should be such that the ball is controlled and directed high into the air so that the player it is directed toward can usefully set the ball up for the next play over the net. With these requisites in mind, the following techniques will have greater meaning for the beginning player.

PHOTO 12. *The Forearm Pass. The forearms are used to make the broadest and flattest area to make contact with the ball.*

Hand Positions

In order to make the forearms a good rebounding surface and to accomplish the required simultaneous contact with the ball, the hands must be clasped together so that both arms act as one. There are four basic handclasps that may be used to achieve this purpose. Each individual player should experiment with them all and select and use the clasp that is personally most comfortable and effective.

The four basic handclasps are:

1. **The Clenched Fist Clasp**

One hand (either one) is clenched into a fist with the thumb facing forward and resting on top of the index finger. The fingers of the other hand are wrapped around the closed fist with the thumbs parallel to one another. When the arms are extended forward and rotated outward, the forearm striking surface becomes apparent. The clenched hands in this position also provide a good rebounding surface should a ball be too low for a clean forearm pass.

2. **Cupped or Curled Finger Clasp**

In this clasp, one hand (either one) is placed palm up into the upturned palm of the other. This starting position is similar to the way one would cup his hands to carry water. The fingers are then curled up so that the thumbs come together, close and parallel to one another. The arms are then extended and rotated outward to form the forearm striking surface.

3. **Thumb-Palm Clasp**

The thumb of the hand closest to the floor (either one) is closed over the top hand. Both palms are facing up. The hands are then hyperflexed downward toward the floor at the wrist. This downward pointing of the hands toward the floor rotates the forearms to the outside creating a broad, flat rebounding surface.

4. **Interlocked Finger Clasp**

The fingers of both hands are interlocked with the thumbs parallel and on top of the intertwined fingers. The arms are then rotated outward by forcing the wrists down, creating a broad contact surface.

With the technique for contacting the ball understood, it now remains for the beginning player to put the forearm pass into play action. To be in proper position for executing the forearm pass, the player must move to a

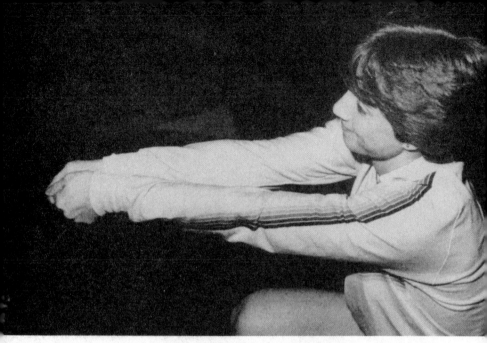

PHOTO 13. *The Clenched Fist Handclasp.*

PHOTO 14. *The Cupped or Curled Finger Clasp.*

PHOTO 15. *The Thumb-Palm Clasp.*

PHOTO 16. *The Interlocked Finger Clasp.*

position directly in front of the incoming ball's line of flight. The idea is to get the center of the body lined up directly in the path of the incoming ball. It is obvious that if the ball is to be played off the exposed flat forearm surfaces of both arms simultaneously, the ball must be contacted along the body's midline. This will ensure contact and prevent "off alignment" hits caused by uneven contact.

Many beginning players have the tendency to reach for the ball with the arms and then try to get into position to make the pass. It is far easier and much faster to get lined up with the ball by using good running and movement techniques—which demand use of the arms—than it is to try to run with the arms in hitting position. It takes far less time to move the arms into good contact position than it takes to move the whole body. The arms also help in maintaining the balance needed to hop, slide, skip, or dance into position. The arms must be first utilized for locomotion, then for striking the ball.

When the player reaches good floor position to receive the ball, the forearms should be brought together and the hands clasped in any one of the ways described. The player should be sure to select the handclasp that is comfortable and allows for the greatest forearm surface exposure, thus providing the greatest amount of control behind the pass. At this point, the entire body is used to play the ball.

With both eyes on the ball and the arms extended out in front of the body, the player bends forward slightly at the waist. The ankles, knees, and hips flex downward slightly to allow for any necessary adjustments caused by changes in the ball's line of flight. Ideally, the ball should be contacted about waist height. Balls that must be played below that height are handled by utilizing the lower body's flex and crouching lower to the floor to get the forearms under the ball.

PHOTO 17. *The Forearm Pass. Both eyes on the ball and the arms extended out in front of the body; the ankles, knees, and hips flex downward slightly.*

It is important to understand that the angle of the forearms will in large part determine the angle and direction of the ball's return. If the forearms are directly perpendicular to the flight of the ball, the ball will trace its original incoming path back away from the passer. By understanding this principle, it is easy for the beginner to see how important it is that all elements that go into the forearm pass make it successful. Getting to the correct spot to play the ball, putting the body and arms into the correct hitting attitude, and using the body to control force and direction all must be in good hitting sequence.

The flex or crouch assumed by the player to adjust to the height of the ball is the same basic method used to add power to passing the ball or to absorb some of the power of hard incoming hits. In the same way that a baseball player cushions the impact of a line drive by letting the arms move back as contact between glove and ball is made, so can the volleyball player absorb some of the power of the hard-hit ball. However, in volleyball the force is not absorbed by the arms alone, but rather by allowing the flex position from the hips through the ankles to "give," shifting some of the force downward and backward as contact is made.

Conversely, to give some added power and drive to softer incoming balls played off the forearms, the player should extend the legs and crouch upward at contact. Force will be provided by the body mass moving up under and behind the arms. The arms should never be swung at the ball to provide force. Obviously vigorous arm swinging would result in hit or miss contact and control would be lost. The applied power would send the ball out-of-bounds up to the rafters or into the net. At the point of contact, the arms should be rigid. Remember, any desired added force applied to the ball or any absorp-

PHOTO 18. *Crouching for Passing. The flex position from the hips through the ankles shifts some of the force downward and backward as contact is made.*

PHOTO 19. *Reaching for Contact with the Ball. The entire body must be turned in the direction of the reach to keep the arms at the desired hitting angle.*

tion of incoming force must be handled by the flex generated by the entire body, up through the legs and into the body itself, not by the arms alone.

It would be ideal to always be in position to play the ball directly in front of the body's midline. However, after reading the chapter on serving and after spending some time actually playing, beginners will soon learn that incoming balls in flight can behave erratically. Some incoming balls will—at the last instant—curve to the left or right, or suddenly rise or drop on the floor, or wobble away from the ideal position of being in front of the body's midline. In these instances it would be virtually impossible to get into the ideal body position. Instead the player will have to reach for the ball. Not simply a desperate stabbing reach, but rather a controlled, compensating reach.

PHOTO 20. *The player plants the foot nearest the ball on the floor with the front shoulder turned forward and down.*

Reaching for contact with the ball still requires the basics of making good contact. The forearm surfaces must be together, the hands must be clasped, and the arms must be rotated outward to present the needed flat contact surface. The key move now is to "reach" the arms into the path of the ball on the angle desired for the return.

To accomplish good contact, the entire body must be turned in the direction of the reach. This will keep the arms at the desired hitting angle. The player plants the foot nearest the ball on the floor, thus establishing the pivot on which the body and arms will turn. With the foot planted, the body is rotated in the same direction with the front shoulder turned forward and down. This will bring the arms into the hitting plane. The body and then the arms are rotated forward to make contact at the point of the intended direction of the pass.

The forearm pass is the basic passing technique employed in volleyball. It takes a great deal of practice in two basic areas: (1) contacting the ball consistently and under control with the forearms, and (2) getting into ideal position so that controlled contact can be made consistently.

This skill can be practiced by players alone against a wall to sharpen the contact phase of the skill. To practice getting into all of the positions from which a player might have to make contact in the course of a game, players should practice passing to one another in pairs, then in groups of three or four. Players will soon be hitting out of semicrouched positions, deep crouched positions, on their knees, and even while sitting on the floor. Since the only method of playing a low ball cleanly is by getting under it, the player must do whatever it takes, and must assume whatever position necessary to get the fists and forearms between the ball and the floor.

SETTING

The set is the refined application of the overhand pass that ideally places or "sets" the ball into position for a spiker to smash home over the net. The set is mainly performed by a player or two who are designated as setters, and whose specific function is setting up the ball for teammates.

Setters are generally selected because of their superior speed, quick reflexes, ability to anticipate play, skill in performing the overhead pass consistently well, and for their leadership and intelligent feeling for the flow of the game. While it is true that the glamor of volleyball often surrounds the leaping, powerful hitting spikers, the key to the spikers' success and to the overall team success is how well the setters perform their passing role. It is far easier to find and develop good spikers than it is to find and develop good setters.

Setters are the quarterbacks of the volleyball team. They begin with their natural ability, then add the necessary technical performance skills. But along with these requisites, they must have an awareness of all facets of the game.

Good setters begin by knowing the ability of their teammates. Each spiker has his own individual strengths and weaknesses, preferences and dislikes, especially when it comes to how and where he wants the ball set up. By tailoring the set to each spiker, based on the particular spiker's strength, setters add immeasurably to the spiker's scoring ability. So, while skill and natural ability are needed, sensitivity and understanding of one's teammates is also important for effective setting.

The second important function of setters is to direct play. This has to do with the setter's ability to "read" and understand the opponent's style of play and counter it through intelligent, well-directed passing. Just like the quarterback in football, the setter must read defenses and pass or give the ball to the correct player in the manner best suited to that particular occasion. When beginning players demonstrate that they possess the natural talent, the desire, and the basic skills necessary to serve as the foundation for good setting, they are ready to learn the refined skill techniques to enable them to carry out aggressive, tactically sound setting.

Good setting is based on refined application of the overhand pass. The overhand pass is a more exact method of controlling the ball because the setter has the opportunity to get positioned under the ball more easily. He or she can watch the ball through the window rangefinder created by proper hand position, and apply control and contact to the ball with the fingertips of both hands.

PHOTO 21. *Setting. To control the ball for the overhand pass, the player should watch the ball approach through the window rangefinder created by proper hand position.*

The key to skillful setting is for the setter to get into good basic position from which the front or back set can be carried out. The setter takes a position with his or her side to the net. Which side—either right or left—is the one closest to the net is contingent upon where the ball is being played from. On occasion, setters even play with their backs to the net. However, this is an advanced skill and not immediately suited to beginning players. Since the setter's main function is to distribute the ball to the right or left spikers, or at times down the middle to set up a player coming from the backcourt, it is obviously unnecessary for the setter to face the opponent's court once the ball has crossed to the setter's side of the court.

Good basic setting position or stance begins with the entire body perpendicular to the net, one foot slightly in advance of the other, the feet approximately shoulder width apart with the knees flexed to assume mobility and balance. The hands and arms are up with the elbows out, and the eyes are on the ball.

Once the setter has moved into position, the opposing team's blockers will be unable to determine whether the setter intends setting the ball forward to the spiker he or she is facing or backward to the player behind the setter. Until the contact point, getting into position for the set and the preparation for the actual contact must consistently appear the same to the opponent to gain maximum setting effectiveness.

The Front Set

The ball has passed over the net. The very next play will usually be a pass to the setter. It is for this reason that effective setters must anticipate the ball's path and move quickly to be positioned under it. When the ball arrives, the setter should be in a stationary, well-balanced posi-

PHOTO 22. *Setting. The skillful setter takes a position with his or her side to the net.*

tion, with the feet in stride position, shoulder width apart with the knees bent. The head is up, the eyes are concentrating on the incoming ball, the arms are up, and the elbows out with the hands up.

The fingers are cupped slightly so that the thumbs and fingertips will contact the ball at the same time. The cupped fingers also keep the ball away from the palms since use of the palms generally results in a ball-handling foul. Just as in the overhand pass, the wrists are flexed backward with the palms facing upward. The index fingers and the thumbs of both hands form the range-finder window through which the setter lines up the flight of the incoming ball. Remember, just as in the overhand pass, the drive and control given the ball comes from the progressive compression or extension of the ankles, legs, hips, shoulders, elbows, wrists, and hands. The hands alone do not do the job.

When contact is about to be made for the front set, the setter takes a slight step back and then forward to make contact with the ball. The ball is contacted with the thumbs and second joints of the index and middle fingers, with the upward thrust provided by the smooth upward extension of the entire body.

The ideal set should place the ball approximately 2 feet from the net and at least 5 feet above the net. The 2-foot distance from the net should be maintained to give the spiker room to operate without making contact with the net or come down under it. Both situations result in a foul and loss of the point or ball.

The 5-foot height above the net gives the spiker the opportunity to time his jump and get high enough into the air to apply explosive downward force with direction.

To achieve good setting techniques, time has to be put into developing good touch at contact. Good touch is designed to put the ball into an arced trajectory, then

PHOTO 23. *The Front Set. The setter takes a slight step back and then forward to make contact with the ball.*

hang for an instant as force behind the ball equals the pull of gravity, resulting in the ball descending nearly straight down into the desired spiking area.

The Back Set

The greatest attribute of the back set is deception. With beginning volleyball players, the front set naturally becomes the most frequently used method of setting up spikers. Just as naturally, opposing blockers will anticipate spikes coming off the front set and move into position to

PHOTO 24. *The ball is contacted with the thumbs and second joints of the index and middle fingers.*

PHOTO 25. *The upward thrust is provided by the smooth upward extension of the entire body.*

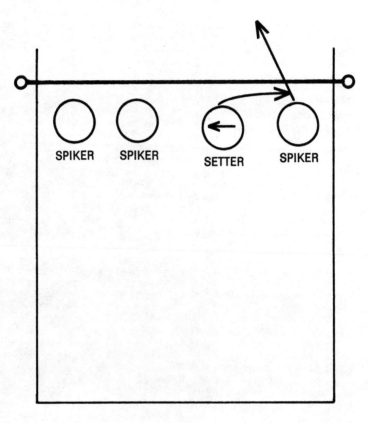

DIAGRAM 8

The Back Set. The setter sets the ball to the spiker behind him, rather than to the spikers the setter is facing.

close down the spike threat. To avoid anticipation of the spike and to keep the blockers off balance, good setters apply the back set.

The key to successful back setting involves employing the same identical movements to get into position and to make contact as in the front set. The variation in direction of the set comes at the moment of contact.

Using the same position up through contact, the player focuses on the incoming ball through the index fingers and thumbs rangefinder. As the ball descends, the setter takes a short step forward, thereby getting further under the ball, arches his back to make contact with the ball above the forehead, and extends the arch and contact backward in the direction of the spiker to the rear. In this way, the ball is actually guided over the head to the rear spiker.

The key to the deception lies in not giving away or "tipping" the direction of the intended pass. Early arching of the back or a rearward glance are directional clues the opponent looks for.

The skilled setter, through peripheral vision, will know which way to pass, front or back. When beginning setters are capable of consistent front and back sets, it is important to devise signals to be given by the setter so that each spiker will be aware of the direction chosen by the setter.

PASSING AND SETTING DRILLS

The main purpose in working hard at passing drills is to get all players reasonably consistent in ball handling. Drills designed for obtaining passing efficiency must progress from simple passes that come from standing almost still to the more complex passes that are made following a run forward, laterally, or even backward.

PHOTO 26. *The Back Set. The player focuses on the incoming ball through the index fingers and thumbs.*

PHOTO 27. *As the ball descends, the setter takes a short step forward, arches his back, and extends the arch and contact backward in the direction of the spiker to the rear.*

PHOTO 28. *The ball is guided over the head to the rear spiker.*

For our purposes, the passing drills are divided into two sections. The first section is concerned with drills to perfect the overhand pass, which by its very nature includes setting drills. Both are related in terms of technique and purpose. The second section is concerned with the forearm pass. While the forearm pass technique is quite different than the overhand, its purpose, in terms of passing, is the same—to play the ball in a controlled and useful manner to a teammate. It is simply not enough to pass the ball *at* another player (except in dire emergencies); the ball must be passed *to* another player with continuity of play possible.

Overhead Passing and Setting Drills

SOLO DRILLS

Solo drills are used by individual players—each with a ball—to get the feel of the ball, work on technique, and get in practice not dependent on having others to practice with. These drills can be done at home, indoors, outdoors, and whenever the player feels the urge to handle the volleyball to perfect individual skills. The player should always begin these drills by concentrating first on assuming the correct arm and hand position (the viewfinder).

Drill #1. Place the ball in the hands in the viewfinder position at about eye level. Toss the ball about 3 feet in the air and then, using good form, pass the ball at a target from 6 to 8 feet above the floor. Choose a spot on a wall or even on the net. The rhythm is ready (ball in starting position), toss, pass to target.

Drill #2. Beginning in the same way as Drill #1, toss the ball in the air, pass it higher, but still close to the starting point, move under the ball, and pass it again. The purpose is to see how long the ball can be kept in the air. Obviously good passing technique must be employed to keep the ball in play.

PARTNER DRILLS

Drill #3. From beginning position, toss the ball low to yourself and then pass the ball slightly above head height to your partner. At first, your partner simply catches the ball using the view-finder technique to watch the ball into his hands. The partners also have the responsibility for checking technique while you are tossing and then passing the ball. The roles reverse and your partner tosses to himself and then passes to you.

Drill #4. A variation of Drill #3 begins with the toss to yourself and then passing the ball on a high trajectory that will allow the ball to drop directly down toward your partner's hand. The partner should then step back allowing the ball to bounce. He then plays the ball off the bounce with a trajectory that allows you to play the ball in the same manner.

Drill #5. One player stands in the center of three or more partners. The drill begins with the toss to yourself and then a pass to one of the players in the ring around you. This player passes the ball to the next player in the ring. Passing continues until the player in the middle has passed to all in the ring. Another player then takes the center position and performs the drill again until all have had a turn or two in the middle.

Drill #6. Two partners set the ball back and forth to one another. Distances between partners should vary between 10 and 15 feet. The trajectory of the sets should vary from high to low, forcing the partner into good position from which to make the set. Keep movement to a minimum at first, concentrating principally on accuracy and having the ball move in a straight down trajectory.

Drill #7. Using the same basics as Drill #6, add a third partner and set two partners on the right and left. The player in the middle is the prime setter, feeding the ball to both partners, who in turn must give a proper set back to the prime setter.

Drill #8. As proficiency in setting develops, work on footwork and movement. This can be done by tossing the ball in the air, setting to yourself, setting to your partner, and moving quickly around your partner. The partner makes the set to you, then runs around you for you to make the set to him again.

Drill #9. In this sitting setting drill, you and your partner sit from 10 to 15 feet apart on the floor. The ball should then be set back and forth between the two of you using only the arms, wrists, and hands. Control is important since movement has been restricted by the seated position.

Forearm Passing Drills

Bearing in mind that the forearm pass must be made from a variety of body positions, drills must incorporate that aspect of movement. However, in the beginning, the keys are (1) getting the handclasp set correctly to expose the forearms for controlled hitting, and (2) getting the body quickly and efficiently into good contact position.

SOLO DRILLS

Solo drills may be used in practicing forearm passing just as they were in the overhand passing drills.

Drill #1. Begin by tossing the ball to yourself, setting the handclasp while the ball is in the air, and then passing the ball into the air or against a wall. Don't be concerned at first with playing the ball again—only concentrate on a controlled first hit.

Drill #2. Toss the ball low in the air, let it bounce, and then pass the ball against a wall.

Drill #3. Face a wall and, off a bounce or toss, pass the ball higher on the wall, move into position, and pass the rebound from the wall back at the wall again. As control develops, strive for 10 consecutive controlled passes against the wall.

PARTNER DRILLS

Partner drills should work in a progressive manner. They should begin simply by one player passing the ball directly back to the partner who tossed him the ball.

Drill #1. Pass to your partner off his tossed bounced ball. The pass should be returned at about the partner's head height, who in turn catches the ball.

Drill #2. Pass to your partner off a directly tossed ball. No bounce is involved. The ball is played in the air. The passer concentrates on giving a useful pass to the tosser.

Drill #3. Partners pass the ball back and forth to one another. The emphasis here must be on control—especially at the beginning. As control increases, movement should be brought into the drills. Restrict movement to a few feet in any direction from the starting point. The height of passes should vary so players can get to bend and develop good movement.

Drill #4. A partner tosses the ball to either side of the passer, making him move into position to pass the ball. This drill will develop good footwork for getting to the ball and emphasize accuracy since the passer must return the ball to the tosser.

Drill #5. Begin with the passer facing two tossers, each with a ball. Tosser one, either of the two, tosses the ball to the passer who returns the ball to the tosser. When the pass is made, the second tosser tosses at the passer, who returns the ball to that passer. As proficiency develops, increase the tempo of the drill to simulate game conditions. Accuracy, footwork, and body position must be stressed as tempo increases. Don't sacrifice accuracy for speed of practice. Instead, build up to speed slowly.

Drill   #6.   Digging serves must also be drilled. Begin
by having a partner or coach serve from 15 to
20 feet away from the passer. It is not necessary to have the net between the server and
the passer. The idea is to get an angle on the
serve that approximates the angle it would
come from if it was passing over the net. The
passer's objective is to return the ball to the
server with a controlled pass.

Drill   #7.   Scramble passing has its place in drill planning. It comes about as a result of well-
placed serves or hits into the vulnerable areas
of the court. Passers line up in playing positions. Other players or the coach throw the
ball anywhere on the court, at varying heights
and speeds. Passers run the ball down, call
out who will make the play, while the closest
other passer backs up or covers the play.

Drill   #8.   Receiving spikes with the forearm pass must
be drilled regularly. The design for drills in
this case must take into consideration the
speed of the ball to be played and passed, as
well as the position close to the floor. Begin
with a partner standing 10 feet from the
passer. The partner, using an overhead throw,
throws the ball at the passer's ankle. The
passer must pass the ball back to the thrower.
As proficiency increases, the partner spikes
the ball from a standing position. The passer
plays the ball back to the thrower.

Drill   #9.   Bring roll and dive techniques into Drill #8
since many passes will be made from these
difficult positions. Practice should begin with

the thrower or spiker telling the passer which way the ball will be coming—to the right or left. The passer should concentrate on getting low, moving to the ball, making controlled contact, completing the dive or roll, and then recovering quickly to get back in the game flow.

Drill #10. A partner or coach stands on a chair or table on one side of the net. Passer or passers are in position on their side of the court. Balls are spiked to passers who return the pass to a setter-catcher whose position on the court may vary. In this way, the passer practices handling the spiked ball by passing it in a controlled manner to the setter. This drill can be performed with a spiker on each side of the court facing two passers. This variation allows for six players at a time to be constructively engaged in this drill.

By keeping in mind the passing demands of play, drills for passing can be designed to meet any specific needs of individuals. These basic drills should serve as a point of departure into developing other drills.

Offensive Attack Skills

THE SPIKE

Without a doubt, the spike contains all the elements that make it one of the most spectacular attacking skills in all sports. The spike ranks with the "slam dunk" in basketball, the overhead smash in tennis, the lightning-fast knockout punch in boxing, and the home run blast in baseball. All have in common the suddenness of the action, the noise of contact, and the most definite finality of result when executed correctly. Virtually every sport has a moment that represents the culmination of skills, tactics, and technique that is designed to finish off the opponent. In volleyball, the skill most frequently representing the culmination of play takes the form of the spike.

Spiking is the name given to the technique of leaping high in the air to drive a ball that has been passed or set above net height into the opponent's court. It is decidedly an attacking play designed, in most cases, to finish off an opponent with great force.

It is apparent that in order to achieve spiking success, timing and coordination must be developed. The spiker must quickly move to spiking position, leap high vertically, time a moving ball coming off a set, make solid contact with the ball, and descend, ready upon contact with the floor to defend against a blocked spike or return. And while all of this is happening, the spiker has to watch his setter, watch the blocks form, and select a high-percentage scoring area to which the ball is to be directed. It's no wonder that the spike represents one of the more difficult skills to coordinate and execute in all sports.

Before getting into the actual skills of spiking, there is a small bit of terminology that applies to spiking, which when understood will add to the beginner's comprehension and subsequent application of actual skills. The two terms used to describe the two different approaches to spiking by an individual player are the on-hand spike and the off-hand spike.

The on-hand spike is performed on what is called the on-hand side of the court. The on-hand side or spike is the side on which the spiker can make contact with the ball with his best or predominant hand *before* the ball crosses his body. If in order to spike the ball with the predominant hand the ball must first cross the player's body, this is called the off-hand spike or the off-hand side of the court.

For example, the left front court corner is the "on-hand side" for a right-handed spiker. The ball to be spiked will be set from the spiker's right, hit by the spiker's right hand, and not cross the spiker's body.

PHOTO 29. *The On-hand Spike. The on-hand side is the side on which the spiker can make contact with the ball with his best or predominant hand before the ball crosses the body.*

PHOTO 30. *The Off-hand Spike. The off-hand side is the side away from the spiker's predominant hand, and the off-hand spike requires that the ball be watched across the body.*

If the same predominantly right-handed spiker is in spiking position at the right front corner of the court, the set ball will come from the spiker's left, and cross his body in order to make contact with the right hand. For left-handed players, the same terminology applies. Whether a ball is taken on-hand or.off-hand is determined simply by whether or not the ball crossed the body before being contacted.

The on-hand spike is generally easier to execute because the spiker can watch his setter as well as the blocks being thrown up at the net while still maintaining visual contact with the ball.

The off-hand spike requires that the ball be watched across the body, thus cutting down on the valuable concentration needed to observe what the defense is setting up.

The reason I point this out is because spiking is best performed by the predominant or strongest arm and hand, but there are some ambidextrous spikers. Since rotation is a basic aspect of the game, each player will have opportunities to spike on his off-hand and on-hand side of the court. Practice must be put into both kinds of spikes, with generally a little more given to the off-hand spike.

Moving into Spiking Position

It is important to note that the spike provides opportunities for each player to bring his or her individual talent and preference into play. While it is true that there are definite components that must be met to execute a winning spike, the steps leading up to actual contact are based largely on individual needs and abilities. Players should be given lattitude in learning the skill building and polishing technique that is based on their natural proclivities.

The starting position for the spiker is somewhere between 8 to 12 feet from the net, close to the sideline. The path the spiker will take will be determined by the setter's position on that particular play. The setter's position in relation to the spiker and the net is the determining factor because it is from that point on the floor that the ball will travel to be in the optimum striking position.

The ideal approach is one in which the spiker can move from his starting position, approaching the net while swinging slightly outside the sideline. This approach keeps the spiker on an angle toward play and where he can keep the setter, the ball, and the blockers in a wide-angle view, all at the same time.

Under less than ideal situations where, for example, the set is coming from deeper into the spiker's court, the spiker should take a wider path to swing farther out-of-bounds before reaching the contact point. The wider swing will present the spiker with a far better angle from which to watch the setter, follow the ball in flight, and a view, albeit a brief one of the defensive alignment.

From the starting position, the beginning spiker makes from three to six strides to approach the contact point. The number of strides necessary may change because of variance in distance to be covered and taking into account outward swing. As in the lay-up shot in basketball, the last step in the approach is taken by the foot opposite to the contact hand. If the spiker is right-handed, the last step prior to takeoff is taken by the left foot. The procedure is reversed for left-handed spikers.

One of the greatest difficulties faced by beginning spikers involves timing for the start of the approach. Most beginning spikers have the tendency to begin the approach to spiking position too soon. This early approach results in the spiker being too close to or even directly under the set. This causes the spiker to have to wait for the set at the net and then jump to contact the ball. The desired momentum of the approach is dissipated, causing a loss in vertical jump height since the spiker must now go up from a standing, stopped position. A further complication caused by an early start and the resulting wait for the ball is that the blockers can now align themselves in such a way to remove the spike threat.

Practice will soon teach the beginning spiker when to begin the approach and the angle to take for the best route to the ball, so that coordination of approach, path, and momentum all blend into an effective vertical jump. Remember, to spike effectively, the ball must be set above the net and the spiker must contact the ball above the net. To accomplish this the approach must become an integral part of the takeoff.

The Takeoff

In order to get height into the vertical jump, the momentum gained during the approach must be redirected from the forward movement into vertical thrust. Forward momentum must be checked to prevent the approaching spiker from contacting the net, which would result in a foul.

The method most often used to achieve vertical height in spiking is called the step-close takeoff. In performing the step-close takeoff, the spiker concludes the approach to spiking position by taking a slightly longer last stride, contacting the floor first with the heel of the lead foot (step) then bringing up the heel of the trailing foot and planting it alongside the front foot (close).

The body is gathered for jump preparation as the feet are being placed in position. The arms are extended backward to nearly shoulder height as the first heel was planted. As the second heel contacts the floor, the arms begin swinging downward in an arc, beginning their upward swing in the arc as the player's weight shifts from the heels to the balls of the feet. The knees are flexed. In one smooth motion the arms thrust up vigorously and the knees extend, lifting the spiker high in the air. The arm thrust is absolutely assential in helping to lift the body from the floor.

As the spiker's arms and hands reach head level, the back should begin to arch backward in a cocked position, in preparation for getting body weight behind the spike. The noncontact arm continues up to nearly full extension above the noncontact shoulder.

The contact arm is cocked at the elbow, thus putting the contact hand into ready striking position behind the head. The upper body twists in the direction of the contact arm with the opposite shoulder turned toward the net. At this point in the spike, the attitude of the upper body is similar to that of a quarterback who is set up to pass, or to the body position of a server in tennis just prior to contact with the ball.

Progression toward contact begins with the non-contact shoulder and arm turning away from the net. The cocked hitting arm begins the path that will bring the hitting hand into contact with the ball, with the elbow leading the way. The contact shoulder and upper torso twist toward the set ball as the body whips forward at the waist.

At contact, the hitting arm is extended and the hand, regardless of striking surface used, is open. The ball should be contacted squarely and crisply above and in front of the hitting shoulder, just at the beginning of the spiker's vertical descent. The follow-through should be close to the body in a downward direction to avoid contacting the net.

PHOTO 31. *The Spike. The takeoff begins with the body gathered for jump preparation.*

PHOTO 32. *With the knees flexed, the arms thrust up vigorously in one smooth motion.*

PHOTO 33. *The contact arm is cocked at the elbow, putting the contact hand in striking position behind the head.*

PHOTO 34. *At contact the hitting arm is extended and the hand is open. Contact should be made squarely and crisply above and in front of the hitting shoulder.*

Contacting the Ball

With a coordinated, well-timed jump, the spiker will be high enough above the set to apply body power to the spike. Since the main purpose of the spike is to forcefully drive the ball down into the opponent's court, a solid striking (contact) surface of the hand must be presented to the ball. The best surface from which to make solid and consistently accurate contact with the ball is the heel of the open hand.

In sequence, the body begins the turn toward the ball, the arm straightens from its cocked elbow position, and the wrist snaps forward, driving the heel of the hand into the ball. The ball should be contacted at or just below its horizontal midline.

A modification in contact can be applied to the ball to give it spin that will cause the ball to drop to the floor in a sharper arc. To apply this spin, the ball is hit by the heel of the hand and the wrist is snapped forward simultaneously. This brings the extended fingers into contact with the ball, imparting spin as the fingers flick down over the ball's surface. This technique is especially useful in spiking balls that are set too far back from the net. In playing balls for spiking that are too far from the net, the spiker must give some arc or trajectory to the hit. When this is done with power, the ball is likely to be driven out of bounds. Therefore, the finger flick is applied to provide the downward arc that results from the applied spin. In this way, power spiking need not be compromised because of distance to be covered.

The Off-Speed Spike

The off-speed spike can be as valuable to a power player as a good change-up pitch is to a fastball pitcher. Both the off-speed spike and the change-up pitch have value only when the opponent is set up, prepared, and expecting a driving power spike.

To the defense, all preliminaries leading up to contacting the ball must be performed exactly as it was in the power spike. The approach, the vertical jump, the body's position in the air, the twist of the trunk, and the cocking of the elbow, wrist, and hand must appear to be geared toward hitting with power.

Since the approach for the off-speed spike to the hit is the same as in the power spike, power has to be removed from the spike by reducing the speed of the hitting arm just prior to making contact with the ball. As players practice hitting the off-speed spike, they will develop and exercise better control over the hitting arm. The longer the spiker can stay in the normal, power spike sequence, the more effective will the change become.

By using a normal approach and a slower arm swing, the spiker will throw off the timing of the blockers. By upsetting the blocker's timing by slowing down the speed of the ball, the backcourt defenders will also come under greater pressure because of the slower hit balls. Backcourt defenders will have to contend with slower balls losing momentum that drop farther in front of them. When defenders compensate for off-speed spiking, it is time to drive the ball hard at them again.

If the spiker uses any other approach method for the off-speed spike, the intention will be telegraphed to the opponents. Alert blockers will immediately detect the change and make the adjustments necessary to counter the off-speed spike. Remember that the off-speed spike is most effective when used sparingly, in order to take advantage of a perceived weakness in the defense, whether that weakness reflects itself in an individual player or in an unprotected area of the court. It is also effective against overly aggressive blockers, since the off-speed breaks the rhythm of their blocks.

PHOTO 35. *The Spike. With a coordinated, well-timed jump, the spiker can apply body power to the spike.*

PHOTO 36. *Progression toward contact begins with the noncontact shoulder and arm turning away from the net.*

PHOTO 37. *The best surface from which to make solid and accurate contact with the ball for the spike is the heel of the open hand.*

THE DINK

The dink is yet another variation of the basic power spike that can be used to break the defender's rhythm by keeping them guessing and, therefore, off balance. Just as in the off-speed spike, the dink is most effective when played off a good set, with blockers and other defenders expecting and prepared for a power spike.

Deception is paramount to executing a winning dink. The preliminary approach for the dink must be exactly the same as in all spiking, as must the takeoff and body attitude. This common approach to the spike keeps the defense guessing while the spiker has the advantage of determining the direction, arc, and velocity to be put on the ball.

The dink is most often executed with the predominant, stronger striking arm. Since all preparation up until contact with the ball is the same, the variation is applied when contact is actually made. In the dink, contact is made with the fingers, not the heel of the hand.

Just prior to contact, arm swing is reduced and the fingertips are used to direct the ball. The wrist may be flicked in the direction of the desired target area. The wrist and fingers in concert can also be used to flick the ball over blockers. It is important that the ball be taken on the fingertips and not the palm.

All spikers should practice dinking the ball for directionality as well as for tipping the ball over blockers. Intelligent use of the dink breaks up blocking rhythms and takes away anticipation from the opponents.

The two-handed variation of the dink can be used to give more impetus and direction, which results in placing the ball deeper into the opponent's court. Both hands must contact the ball at the same time. Two-handed dinks are especially useful when rebounding a ball that returns to the spiker's side of the court as a result of a successful block.

Beginning players will have the tendency to try to smash every spike attempt. Control must come before power, and control is built on body control, timing, and coordination. The glamor of the spike draws beginners into mistakenly wanting to hit with too much power too soon. Most spiking practice time must be devoted to developing the approach, strengthening the takeoff, getting the body into the shot, and deciding which spike to employ in a given situation. Power will come with refined technique. Consistent spiking success results from being able to vary the spike at will.

SPIKING DRILLS

Designing drills for spiking presents an interesting challenge to both the coach and the players. Since the actual spike is performed while the spiker is airborne, drills must be designed to practice getting into the air as well as for actual contact with the ball.

The things that spiking drills should try to accomplish are:

1. Powerful leg thrust to lift the player above the net
2. A well-timed, controlled approach to the spiking position
3. A forceful spike or well-placed dink, depending upon the opportunity presented by the defensive blockers
4. Coordination of the entire play

PHOTO 38. *The Dink. Contact with the ball is made with the fingers, not the heel of the hand, and the fingertips direct the ball.*

PHOTO 39. *The Two-handed Dink. The fingertips of both hands must make contact with the ball at the same time. The two-handed variation gives the ball more impetus and direction, putting the ball deeper in the opponent's court.*

Therefore, these drills should serve as a basis for designing further drills as the needs of players become more apparent. As players' skills become more polished and they are able to perform more complex moves, drills for these new variations will have to be designed.

Approach Drills

Approach drills, as with all other drills, should begin after a thorough warm-up. Spiking drills call for vigorous extension of the entire body, stretching muscles, ligaments, and joints. Here is where flexibility exercises and warm-up will pay off.

The entire squad can work on these approach drills at the same time. Partners pair off for spiking drills later on.

Drill #1. Practice the rock-jump using no approach. Stand close to the net or a wall that has the net height painted on it. Without an approach, the player rocks back on the heels, flexes the knees to a semisquat, then rocks forward while swinging the arms forward and up vigorously. The legs are extended for the jump. Jump. Check height above the net height. The rock-jump should be repeated 20 to 30 times.

Drill #2. Next the step-close jump approach should be practiced. The player takes one step forward with the preferred jumping leg, plants it, brings up the trailing leg, rocks forward from the heels, and jumps vertically. Practice 20 to 30 times.

Drill #3. After Drills #1 and #2, each spiker should be ready for running approach practice. This drill is aimed at putting running movement into the takeoff. Players should practice the approach from the right, middle, and left areas of the court. Employ the number of steps needed to get to the spiking point, plant the takeoff leg, and jump high vertically. Repeat 15 to 30 times, alternating starting positions on the court.

Combined Approach and Spiking Drills

Drill #4. With a partner standing on a chair holding a ball well away from the body, the spiker approaches and spikes the motionless ball into the opposite side of the court. This drill should be used as a culmination to Drills #1, #2, #3. It sets the timing for the jump, allows the player to leap, cock the spiking arm, get the entire body into the contact, and make the actual contact. Repeat 10 to 20 times.

Drill #5. This drill is an action drill, which means that the spiker will be attacking a moving ball that has been either set or tossed. First, spike a tossed ball. Second, spike a ball that has been set. Setters should be employed in this second part of the drill since both the spiker and the setter can practice at the same time for mutual benefit. Work slowly at first to coordinate approach timing and the jump so that contact is made crisply, well above the net. The number of repetitions depends upon the need of the individual spiker. It is ideal to get 10 to 20 consecutive good spikes from each of the two drill formats. You will soon learn that the tossed ball travels in a flatter trajectory than does the well-executed set. By working with both kinds of passes, the toss and the set, the spiker is given greater game simulation.

Drill #6. Use the same drill formats as in Drill #5 with tossed and set balls to practice on-hand as well as off-hand spiking. Spikers must be prepared for the different perspectives and adjustments for taking the spike from both sides.

Drill #7. Spikers must also drill on spiking balls that come from various places on the court. To practice, the spiker should take position, in turn, at all three net, front court spiking positions. The ball should be set or tossed from the right, left, and center of the court. Tosses or sets should come from normal setting positions as well as from behind or more difficult areas of the court. The spiker will be forced to develop proper movement to get into spiking position.

Drill #8. When spiking consistency is developed, it is time to work on spiking accuracy. To accomplish this, targets such as traffic cones, chairs, or towels should be placed on the other side of the court. The ball is then set to the spiker who tries to hit a specific target.

Drill #9. As skill and accuracy develop, Drill #8 can be practiced with first one and then two blockers. The spiker now practices "beating" the block and is given the options of spiking through or around the block, dinking, or using an off-speed spike to beat the block. Blockers are, at the same time, practicing their blocking skills.

Drill #10. At the conclusion of practice, a 3–5 minute jump rope program should be used. While jumping rope is an excellent conditioning drill, it also lends itself to spiking and blocking practice since the player is forced to jump, land, jump—as spiking and blocking demand in the course of play.

Defensive Techniques

BLOCKING

In volleyball terminology, blocking is the term given to the aggressive defensive play of one or more players at the net whose purpose it is to intercept the ball, thwarting the opponent's attack. All players in the front line are eligible blockers. Blockers are permitted to reach as far over the net as possible, provided they do not come into contact with the ball before the opponents have played it or with the net during play.

While blocking is considered the front line of the defense and taught as a defensive technique, through practice and proper execution of the skill, it can be turned into offensive, attacking volleyball that results in scoring points.

Good blocking technique also provides ancillary benefits to overall team success. Aggressive, effective blocking can have a strong psychological effect on opposing spikers. Effective blocks put a great deal of pressure on spikers, causing them to alter their hitting technique, hesitate while selecting their target areas, become intimidated (forcing them into attempting low-percentage spikes), or by having their spikes jammed back down their throats. Whatever the effect of good blocking on each individual spiker, the important thing is that whatever the spiker intends to do with impunity should be altered by aggressive blocking. When aggressive blockers can achieve this goal, the added pressure put on the spiker will result in points for the blocking team.

Starting Position

For blocking to be effective, the blocker must be able to get both hands above and over the net without making contact with the net. Tall players or good jumpers generally assume a starting position approximately a full arm's length away from the net. In taking this starting position, all thrust generated upward from the floor, necessary to get above the net, is vertical—keeping the blocker away from the net.

In the case of beginning blockers, as well as shorter or less capable leapers, more momentum must be put into the takeoff to achieve greater height. Experience in other sports and play activities has taught us that it is possible to get more lift into a jump if we use a run up to take off, which is also called the approach to takeoff. The basic problem in utilizing a running approach is that very often the forward momentum generated in the approach is carried into the vertical liftoff. While in the running long jump this is desirable, it is not so in volleyball, since going forward would put the blocker into the net, resulting in a foul.

Realistically, beginning players, shorter players, and average jumpers will need to add a boost to their jumping ability. While this boost can be gained through physical conditioning, leg-strengthening exercises, and drills, effective blocking can be aided by understanding the technique and development of a concentrated and controlled vertical leap, even when coming off a short runing approach.

Footwork for the Approach and Takeoff

When the run is employed by blockers, it generally starts several feet back from the net. Naturally, the run and takeoff take better timing, coordination, and concentration (and more practice) than simply being able to leap high vertically while standing an arm's length from the net. Therefore, the fewer number of steps the blocker has to take before the vertical takeoff, the better the chances for effective blocking. Try to limit the approach to four steps.

The first step in the approach should be taken with the inside foot, or the foot toward the middle of the court. The last step should be taken on the outside foot. The reason the outside foot should be planted last is so the body will come into position facing the spikers and the opponent's court squarely. This positioning of the body cuts down on the blocker's tendency to fade or lean toward the outside of the court. By facing the opponents squarely the blocker can observe the opposing setter's preparation for the set and look for position for the block. Also, any fade to the outside in approach or takeoff will take the blocker farther away from a teammate, whose blocking assistance is always needed. By moving away from teammates, gaps are created that can be easily exploited by the spiker should the block fail.

Takeoff

The gathering in of the body for the takeoff is similar to the takeoff technique described in the spike. When the heel of the outside foot is planted, the inside foot is drawn up alongside, the knees are flexed, and the arms are extended backward, hands pointing toward the floor at almost shoulder level.

As the weight of the body begins the transfer from the heels to the balls of the feet, the arms are swung down and then forward, helping lift the blocker from the floor. The knees extend sharply at the same time. This smooth, coordinated flow, combining transfer of weight, arm swing and lift, and leg extension is what lifts the blocker high in the air. The coordinated movements will come only as a result of practice.

If less of a run is needed or if only one step is needed, as in the case of better or taller blockers, the blocker first moves to the takeoff point. At this point, the knees are flexed and the arms are drawn back in preparation for their contribution to the lift. The blocker's head should be up watching the setting preparation of the opponents. All bend and flex in the body at this point is in the knees. The back is straight since no body whip is intended to be added to the block.

As the jump is started, the elbows are swung back, with the body's weight on the heels. At the jumping instant, the weight is transferred to the balls of the feet, the arms are swung forward and up vigorously, and the knees extend, lifting the blocker from the floor. The arms go straight up with the hands close enough together to prevent the ball from passing between them. The hands should be extended with the fingers spread to cover as much of the ball as possible. The arms are close to the net with the wrists exerting the force necessary to put the ball back into the opponent's court.

PHOTO 40. *Blocking. The takeoff for the block is similar to that for the spike. As the weight of the body begins the transfer from the heels to the balls of the feet, the arms are swung down and then forward, helping lift the blocker from the floor.*

After contact with the ball, the hands and arms must be drawn back quickly to avoid contact with the net. The descent from blocking is absorbed by the balls of the feet and the cushioning effect of the knee flex. In this way, the blocker lands in a well-balanced position, ready and in control to continue play.

Utilizing More than One Blocker

Team blocking means exactly what it implies. More than one player will contribute to the block. It would be ideal to be able to have all three potential blockers at the net involved in a well-coordinated team attempt to stop a spiker, but this is rarely the case. Volleyball is simply too fast a game to allow three players enough time to gang

PHOTO 41. *The knees extend sharply, and the combined transfer of weight, arm swing and lift, and leg extension is what lifts the blocker high in the air.*

PHOTO 42. *The arms should go straight up with the hands close enough together to prevent the ball from passing between them. The fingers should be spread to cover as much of the ball as possible.*

up at a particular spot on the net, especially at either of the corners. It is conceivable that three blockers could converge in concert, on occasion, at the center of the court, but those occasions are rare, since most spikes are not aimed for the center of the court. Therefore, most team blocking opportunities will involve two blockers.

In two-player team blocking, the player closest to the play of the ball determines the positioning of the block. At either corner of the court, the end player or blocker establishes floor position first, with responsibility following then to the middle blocker to move laterally to join forces.

The end blocker's chief responsibility, whether on his own or in tandem with the center blocker, is to close off the sideline area to the spiker. This is accomplished by blocking from a position close enough to the sideline to cut the angle to the line. The end blocker invariably positions himself outside the spiker to take away the side line spike or to prevent any partially blocked rebounds of the blocker to go irretrievably out of bounds. The idea is to force the ball into where there is the greatest concentration of team-mates, where help is readily available. The middle blocker provides the coverage to the inside, closing off spiking lanes into the middle.

The front line players should always attempt to throw up at least a two-blocker defense. Four hands properly positioned and high in the air will do much to cut down spiking angles. This gives the opponent much less in terms of free access to the court. These blocking tactics, when properly executed, force spikers into adjustments they don't want to make and result in errors on the spiker's part.

If by chance, and it is much more likely to occur with beginners than advanced players, a situation arises in which there is the opportunity for three blockers to be employed against a spiker, remember that areas left open by players engaged in the block are extremely vulnerable to the dink. Backcourt players must anticipate vacancies that occur due to blocking assignments and fill these open areas quickly. They must be alert for the inevitable counter to the blocks that have been set up.

BLOCKING DRILLS

Blocking drills are designed to give practice in three main areas:

1. The block itself with practice aimed at the individual player blocking effectively and legally
2. Team blocking where two or more players combine to execute the block together
3. Building and increasing anticipation and reaction time for setting the blocks whether the block is performed individually or in tandem with a teammate

A thorough warm-up should be taken prior to performing blocking skills since blocking requires quick movement to get into position, explosive vertical jumping, and great overall body extension. A complete warm-up, with an emphasis on flexibility of all joints, will prevent muscle pulls and strains.

It must also be remembered that effective blocking comes from a good, high vertical jump with the flex coming from the shoulders rather than the hips, as it does in spiking. Get the arms and hands high. Shoulder flex will provide this, but flexing from the hips will decrease height. Both hands and arms must be brought into the block. Therefore, the shoulders must provide the power base while the blocker is in the air.

PHOTO 43. *Two-player Blocking. The end player (left) establishes position first to close off the sideline area to the spiker.*

PHOTO 44. *The middle blocker (right) provides the coverage to the inside, closing off spiking lanes in the middle.*

PHOTO 45. *Four hands properly positioned and high in the air will do much to cut down spiking angles.*

Solo and Partner Drills

Drill #1. Begin by practicing the take off with the rock-jump technique. Blocking doesn't allow the time for long approaches, as does the spike. Blockers must move quickly into position and explode into the air at the correct instant. Start standing close to the net. Rock back on the heels, flex the knees to a semisquat, rock forward while both arms swing up, extend the legs vigorously, and jump. At the top of the jump, flex the outstretched arms and hands over the net to form an umbrella over imaginary spikers. Bring arms and hands back quickly, so as not to contact the net. Land in balance ready to go up again. When this basic, simple drill is mastered, it can be improved upon by having players repeat 10 times in succession. Technique should be stressed at all times.

Drill #2. To build upon previous drills and to begin to develop control and placement, players should take the same starting position at the net. Holding a ball in both hands the player should jump, extend hands and arms with elbows locked, and, using wrist action only, throw the ball to the floor. Practicing this motion, which uses the wrists to throw the ball, approximates the technique used in actual blocking. Perform this drill 10 to 15 times.

Drill #3. To add some gamelike conditions to Drill #2 and to apply some real blocking, place one player on each side of the net. Each pair consists of a thrower and a blocker. Using the technique described in Drill #2, the thrower jumps and tries to throw the ball over the net as if spiking. The partner moves into position and attempts a solo block on the thrown ball. Each player should take a turn, with the blocker becoming the thrower and the thrower becoming the blocker. As the players get better at the technique, they can play 11-point games between each other, with only successful blocks winning points.

Beginning Action Blocking Drills

At the propitious moment, blockers will have to go up against real spikers. Preparation for this phase must be built gradually to reinforce technique, keep timing sharp, and to be sure blockers become aggressive and yet controlled.

Drill #1.   Using a partner who will actually spike the ball, blocker goes up for the block in a one-on-one situation. The spiker may spike from a set made to him or may set the ball up to himself and then spike over the net. Each partner should take 10 to 15 spikes or blocks in a row and then alternate.

Drill #2.   Another method of intensifying blocking practice against more consistent spiking is to put a partner on a chair, which eliminates the jump since he is now above the net. The spiker spikes the ball straight over the net. The blocker must attack the spiked ball with a solid block. Repeat 10 to 15 times and exchange roles with your partner.

Drill #3.   To practice team blocking, put one player on a chair to ensure consistent spiking. With two blockers you are forced to move into area blocking with the blocker closest to the sideline being the main blocker and his teammate the backup. The spiker on the chair directs the ball at either of the two blockers, who must react with area coverage for one another. Repeat 10 to 15 times and alternate players in the spiking position and as the blocker, beginning on the left. In this way, the complete cycle among three players will give 30 to 45 blocking situations to each individual.

Drill #4. To add real zest to Drill #3, set up three chairs with three spikers, each with a ball. Each spiker should be numbered 1, 2, or 3. On the other side of the net, set three blockers in normal game position. A coach or a manager calls out a number. The spiker whose number is called spikes the ball over the net with the appropriate pair of blockers reacting in an attempt to make the block. The only clue the blockers have is which of the spikers will be spiking. As it is in a game, the clue or tip as to which spiker will actually spike the ball, comes just seconds before the spike. Blockers must react quickly and go up for the block. Immediately after the play, another number is called with the blockers having to react to the new situation. Six players at a time can be involved in this drill. Blockers have 15 to 20 blocking attempts before they exchange places with spikers.

Drill #5. Blocks should also be practiced against passed balls coming over the net. On many occasions, the return over the net will not be a spike. To practice blocking against this possibility, have a partner throw the ball over the net. The blocker then must go in the air and block the thrown ball.

Drill #6. There will be occasions when an apparent block can be turned into a spike that will result in a score. A miscue on a spike or dink may present the blocker the opportunity of changing the intended block to a spike. To practice for this eventuality, have a partner toss the ball over the net. The blocker goes up as if to block, perceives the change in plan, and corrects the body and arm motion into a spike. The key factor here is not simply the spike, but rather the opportunity that is presented when the block was apparently called for. Practice this drill 10 to 15 times.

Drill #7. Not all blocks are cleanly successful. Often the block is attempted by one player in the pair with the result being that the ball is partially blocked, but doesn't stay on the opponent's side of the net. In this situation, the covering player must dig for the ball. This becomes complicated because the blocker had been in the air for the block and now has to dive for the dig. This can be practiced by having the blocker go up for the block then turning toward his partner, diving and digging for a tossed ball.

All blocking drills should be practiced hard. Attacking, aggressive blocking provides for intimidation of spikers, which seriously can affect spiking technique.

DIGGING

Spiking is sensational and blocking is essential, but digging is both sensational and essential in its contribution to winning volleyball. Let us first understand the term without getting too far into semantics. Obviously, the serve, spike, and block have been designed to get the ball to the court floor (on the opponent's side) before the opponent has a chance to prevent that from happening. If the ball does get to the floor within the court boundary lines, it costs the team a point.

"Dig" is the term applied to getting the defender's arms and/or hands into effective passing position somewhere between the descending ball and the floor, thus keeping the ball in play. In order to achieve proper hitting surfaces between the ball and the floor, the player must "dig" for the ball. The player must, in effect, reach under the ball in a manner analogous to placing a shovel under sand, snow, dirt, etc., and lift the material or, in this case, the ball, up and away.

In continuing the analogy between the volleyball dig and shoveling, the flat surface of the shovel's blade becomes the hands and arms, and the rest of the body and its function in digging is similar to the shovel handle.

Digging demands players that are aggressive, determined, and unafraid of going to the floor to get under the ball to prevent contact with the floor. The skills needed for controlled contact with the floor are learned skills that can be safely practiced until they become part of each player's techniques. But successful digging begins with desire and competitive drive. If a player begins with these two traits, the skill of digging can be effectively and safely mastered.

PHOTO 46. *The Dig. The defender must get his arms and/or hands somewhere between the descending ball and the floor and must often "dive" for a dig.*

Technique of the Dig

In the basic preparatory stance for digging, the player assumes a position similar to that of a defensive basketball player. The feet and legs are spread, with one foot slightly in advance of the other, giving the player both balance and mobility. The player's weight rests on the balls of the feet with the knees bent. Hands and arms are in front of the body at about waist height, with the overall posture being slightly forward.

In assuming this basic stance in preparation for digging, it is important to remember that, once more, individual preferences come into play as far as instant mobility is concerned. The actual stance assumed should recognize the elements involved in the basic stance yet should be adapted to the individual player's ability to move, stay low, and get the arms into good contact position. Therefore, the stance assumed should be one that allows the digger enough mobility to get to the ball and then to get as much of the digger's body in front of and perpendicular to the ball's incoming line of flight. In this way greater control and accuracy will be present at contact.

Beginning players should use the basic forearm pass for digging whenever possible. The forearm pass allows

PHOTO 47. *Digging demands players that are aggressive, determined, and unafraid of going to the floor to get under the ball to prevent its contact with the floor.*

the greatest and flattest contact surface, giving optimum control under the most difficult passing conditions.

The idea of the dig is to make a playable pass to a teammate, generally a setter, and not to return the ball over the net. If players understand this, then the objectives of the dig, in terms of performing the skill, relate directly back to the basic skills described in the forearm pass.

As the player moves into position to execute the dig, the hands are clasped with the elbows and arms fully extended. The arms are rotated to the outside to expose more forearm surface area. The ball should contact the arms on the exposed forearms just above the wrists. When contact is made properly, the digger is able to place the ball higher in the air to the designated setter. Here is where use of the arms is brought into play.

Slow-paced balls require that the digger get under the ball, make contact, and move the arms upward in tandem, in the intended direction of play. Lift will not as easily be applied to the ball as it is in less stressful passing situations since the rest of the body will be dropping or rolling toward the floor. By getting the arms as close to parallel to the floor as possible, the arms can be raised to provide the desired lift without imparting too much unwanted forward directionality to the ball. Controlled lifting of the ball to a teammate is the objective. The resulting pass that comes directly from a dig must be playable or else it was wasted effort.

When digging a hard-driving ball that comes off a well-hit serve or spike, the arms do not move at all even though the rest of the player's body is in a frenzy of motion. If arm life were added to the already fast-paced incoming ball, the rebound would result in an uncontrolled pass of no use to anyone but the opponent.

In this instance, the digger must cushion the impact of hard-driving spikes to retain control of the pass. (See the

PHOTO 48. *Digging Stance. As the player moves into position to execute the dig, the hands are clasped with the arms and elbows fully extended. The arms are rotated to the outside to expose more forearm surface area.*

chapter on passing.) The cushioning effect is achieved by absorbing the blast on the arms at contact by allowing the knees, hips, and body to flex or give in a downward direction. The idea is to "give" in the direction the ball is going. It is, however, a bit more difficult to find room to give when in close proximity to the floor. It is apparent that methods of safely digging the ball close to the floor and recovering quickly enough to continue play have to be examined.

Contacting the Floor

I have deliberately avoided the term "hitting the floor," because that is precisely what the digger does not want to do. Good diggers contact the floor in such a manner that the more rounded, meatier portions of the body cushion any impact and allow the body's momentum to roll over the floor rather than drive into it. Appendages such as arms, legs, and head must be tucked into the body so that they will not provide any resistance to the roll. Tucked-away appendages are far less likely to be strained, bent, or broken during the rolling contact process.

THE BACKWARD ROLL

The backward roll is most appropriate when used to play an incoming ball that forces a passer to move backward, getting into a deep crouch to get under the ball or to cushion a hard-driving spike. The momentum of the backward move to position flows into the deep crouch necessary to keep the arms in position under the ball.

As contact is made, the player sits back softening the impact with the floor by contacting the floor on one buttock and then bringing the legs up in line with where the momentum is taking the body. The chin is tucked to the chest, the back curved to make the roll easier, and the knees tucked up into the chest as the roll backward continues.

If momentum is great, continue the roll up onto the shoulders and finish with a simple back somersault. The correct finish to the backward roll has the player emerge from the roll facing the net.

With less momentum, a backward somersault is not needed. What the player should do is allow his body to rock up on a curved back position up to the shoulders, and let the legs come up toward the chest with the knees bent. At the top of the roll, when momentum is lost, the legs should be brought down while the body comes down the back arch. The feet are placed under the body and the hands and arms push against the floor to bring the player to a standing position.

Recovery from the roll must be rapid to keep the player in the game, but it is just as important to complete the roll. All or as much momentum as possible must be dissipated for safety's sake. Sudden stops in the roll are likely to cause injury.

The best way to practice backward roll techniques is to do rolls without a ball, at first, on grass, sand, or gymnastic mats. When practicing the backward roll the most important thing to concentrate on is staying low to avoid hard impact at contact with the floor and to let the roll flow through to its conclusion. Conscientious practice will make the backward roll become second nature so that concentration then can be directed at playing the ball.

THE SIDE ROLL

The side roll is the culmination of a dig made after a run to the far right or left to contact the ball. The run or reach

PHOTO 49. *The Backward Roll. As contact is made, the player sits back, softening the impact with the floor by contacting the floor on one buttock and then bringing the legs up. The chin is tucked to the chest, the back curved to make the roll easier, and the knees tucked up into the chest as the roll backward continues.*

to get into good contact position will keep the player's momentum going in that same direction. The trick in getting a good pass out of a difficult side dig is keeping the arms in a level plane, parallel to the floor and up, until contact with the ball is made. This is accomplished by staying low, with the legs spread wide, moving crablike to the ball. In this way, the player's center of gravity remains under him for a longer time, making ideal contact possible.

At the point of contact, the player's lead knee (the one on the side the player is moving toward) should drop to the floor. This is one of the reasons why many players choose to wear rubber and elastic knee pads. The knee on the floor provides a stable base from which to pass as well as a pivotal point around which the player rolls.

After contact with the ball, the momentum carries the player into a controlled roll. Both knees are now fully bent with the thigh on the side in which direction the player was going becoming the cushion for the roll. Both arms are tucked in close to the body so that no parts stick out to interrupt the flow of the roll.

The player then rolls around, over the thigh onto the buttocks and onto the curved back and shoulders. The player's head will be aimed at the net. As momentum continues, tuck the knees in and roll onto the opposite thigh and start coming up, using the hands and arms if needed. When done smoothly and quickly, the player is back into playing position in seconds.

The side roll can be practiced on sand, grass, or gymnastic mats. Like the backward roll, the side roll is designed to prevent injury by allowing generated momentum to be dissipated through movement and flow rather than by sudden braking. Either roll allows safe, injury-free conclusions to different plays.

Basic Team Concepts

One of the joys found in playing volleyball is that it is a team sport. Whether played casually on a beach, in a park with friends, or in competition on any level where the game is taken more seriously, teamwork is the essential ingredient, not only to success, but to the actual enjoyment of the game.

As in all team sports, the success and overall effectiveness of the team is predicated on the interrelationship and coordination of the natural athletic ability, skill, function, and responsibilities of each team member. Each player on a team is dependent upon the other, and each individual bears responsibility not only for himself, but for the other team members as well.

In any team sport a player is often able to pull off a great individual feat on a particular play, but the prelude to that play was performed by one or more teammates. In

PHOTO 50. *Successful volleyball is based on the interrelationship and coordination of the abilities, skills, and responsibilities of each team member. Here a team is properly set to receive the ball from their opponent.*

volleyball, a well-driven scoring spike simply does not happen without a controlled, accurately placed set. While the relationship of the two players in this example is apparent, what is not so apparent is that in order for a player to have set the perfect pass, another team member had to pass the ball to the setter in a way that made the perfect set possible. Three individuals had to participate in the winning spike.

Every practice session and game will present new situations and demands requiring appropriate responses from each member of the team. Therefore, in order to be a contributing member of the team, each player must:

1. Develop, practice, and refine his or her individual skills
2. Develop an understanding of the functions and responsibilities of his or her own positions *and* those of teammates
3. Develop a thorough understanding of the team's system of play
4. Train hard physically to be able to execute skills on a high level throughout a game without fatigue, which can cause weakness in play
5. Make the maximum effort in his or her position and to teammates at all times

These are the necessary ingredients to bring to any system of play.

Developing a team's style of play is not an easy task. A system of play must be determined by an honest evaluation of each player in terms of the realistic contribution each can make to the overall team effort. Systems and tactics are based on the following:

1. Skill levels of individuals
2. Overall skill levels of the team as individuals complement each other
3. Speed, quickness, and agility
4. Court sense—mental responses in handling varied and ever-changing play situations
5. Physical condition
6. Age level

While all of these factors are important in designing an overall offensive and defensive style of play, specific basic and fundamental concepts are the foundation for most volleyball tactics and systems of play. Before more sophisticated systems can be introduced, the beginning player and team must understand these basic concepts. When an individual and a team have mastered individual skills and blended their skills into team play consistently, more advanced concepts can be added. Indeed, teams that function well will find more advanced concepts coming from within themselves.

FUNDAMENTAL TEAM PLAY

The classic and most basic passing pattern in volleyball is aimed at providing opportunities to spike the ball for a winner. The spike is the number one offensive attack weapon. Therefore, the basic pass pattern, utilizing fundamental passing skills, is designed to get the ball into perfect spiking position.

As the ball is played from the opponent's court over the net, whether on a serve, a volley return, a spike, or a block, the first move should be to pass the ball, under control, to the setter positioned in the center front court near the net. The setter then sets the ball—to either the left or right front court player positioned at the intersection of the net and sideline—depending on the defensive alignment, for the spike. The spiker then slams the ball home into the opponent's court. The pass-set-spike pattern of play is the foundation for building all other volleyball offensive options.

The first hit after the ball has come over the net is usually played with a forearm pass. The basic pass-set-spike pattern calls for this pass to be directed to the center of the front court at a height of 3 to 6 feet above the net. The ball is passed high to allow the setter time to get into position. The setter should be looking in the direction of the passer, while adjusting his position so that the set can

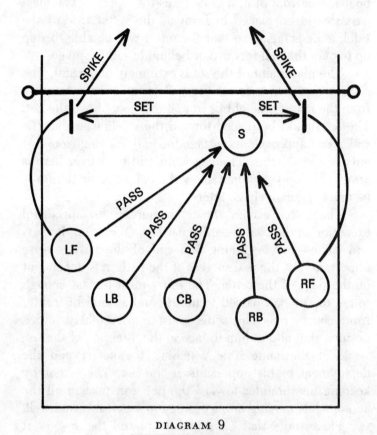

DIAGRAM 9

Pass-Set-Spike Pattern and Rhythm of Play.

be made in front of him as he faces the sideline. The ideal pass should be placed in front of the setter toward the sideline he is facing so that the setter will be able to step up to play the ball forward or behind to either spiker.

The placement of the set is extremely important. The setter's objective is to set the ball from 1 to 2 feet away from the net at a height of from 4 to 6 feet above the net. The set should be placed toward the sideline so that the spiker can approach and attack the ball, starting from just outside the sideline. The key word and maneuver here is *attack*. The spiker cannot allow the ball to come to him— he must aggressively go after it.

The setter carries the main burden for successful execution of the pass-set-spike pattern. Of course, the pass and spike—the beginning and end of the pattern—are important, but the real success of the pattern is dependent on the skills of the setter. The setter must be fast enough to get to any ball passed to him in and around his center front court area. The setter must move quickly into a position that allows him to face in the direction of the set, while at the same time watching the passer and the deployment of his opponents at the net. The setter, by keeping his shoulder toward the net, can take in all the action while moving into a position to set cleanly and well.

Please note that I specifically placed the spikers at the corners of the court at the net. While it is possible and sometimes practical and desirable to spike from midcourt, beginning players who are just mastering control of the spike need all the help they can get. The left and right front court positions near the intersection of the sideline and net give beginning spikers hitting angles that present the greatest distance to the opponent's sidelines. The greater space created by playing the angles gives beginning spikers a smaller margin for error until control of the ball is sharpened.

From either corner, the spiker has three options: (1) spiking down near the sideline; (2) spiking diagonally across to the far opposite corner of the court; and (3) spiking to the sideline opposite the spiker's side of the court. (See Diagram 10.) Each spike line gives the beginning spiker more area to aim for, as opposed to spiking from center net.

Of course, all of the foregoing pass-set-spike tactics are contingent upon a well-executed pass, a well-executed set, and a well-executed spike. It is easy to theorize on paper, planning and plotting the path of the ball, but in active play many variables enter into each and every situation that result in less than accurate, diagramlike passing.

Inaccurate passing forces deviation from the basic plan and compels teams to pursue alternate plans of play. It is important to point out that while beginning players and teams are most vulnerable to passing inaccuracies, advanced players and teams are also vulnerable, albeit with less frequency. Recognition of a beginner's tendencies toward less than accurate passing leads to the development of alternative plans. Practicing contingency plans will prepare teams for coping with less than optimum game situations. They also provide the foundation for building a more varied approach to team techniques as skills improve in individual players.

For example, in an instance where it is difficult to get to a ball coming over the net, an inaccurate pass may result. Ideally, the ball would have to be passed to the center front setter who turns it over to either flanking spiker. If the inaccurate pass is off the center setter target, it will have to be played by either the left or right spiker.

To get back to the flow of the pass-set-spike tempo, the left or right corner spiker should call off the setter by saying something like "Stay!," "I've got it!," or "My ball!"

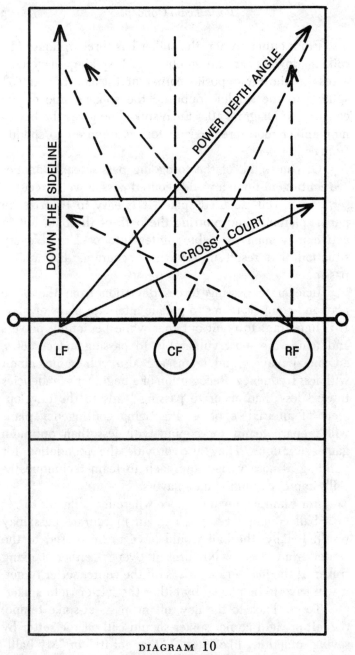

DIAGRAM 10

Spiking Angles.

The corner spiker should attempt to set the ball to the opposite side spiker by using a crosscourt set. This way the rhythm of play is preserved. The movement of the ball crosscourt forces the blockers to react and move with the play and prevents them from setting blocks on their terms.

If passes are kept in the backcourt because of difficulty in playing them cleanly and in a controlled manner, then backcourt players, by necessity, become responsible for setting the ball to a front court spiker. If the first pass doesn't get the ball to the front court area, then the next pass, regardless of which player in the backcourt is involved, again by necessity, should ideally be a set. The set from the backcourt should be to a spiker diagonally opposite the setter. That way it will be easier for the spiker to make the spike from a diagonal pass from behind.

Variations on the basic pass, set, and spike are many and are always dictated by the flow of the game. Sometimes the three-part sequence is stopped at two when an exceptional opportunity to spike comes from a super pass. The point of being prepared for all contingencies is that breaking the basic rhythm can sometimes be a way of scoring quickly, provided that the rhythm breaking is used intelligently, especially when the opponent is caught off guard and, therefore, is most vulnerable to surprise.

OFFENSIVE STRATEGY

Volleyball, like soccer and basketball, is a game of rapid transition. Transition, in sports terminology, generally refers to the smooth, rapid change of ball possession from one team to the other. In all team sports, the team in possession of the ball is attacking and therefore on the offensive, while the team without the ball is defending. In general, this mode of thinking is correct for most sports, but in volleyball, offense and defense are not so easily defined.

For example, the team serving the ball is most definitely on the offensive. With a well-driven, well-placed serve into the opponent's backcourt, the opponent, now in possession of the ball (figuratively), may be playing the ball defensively just to keep it in play. At this moment, the team in possession of the ball can hardly be said to be on the attack.

Therefore, let us be sure to understand that because of the rapidity of play, which results in the ball's changing sides of the court so frequently, it becomes extremely difficult to determine when defensive or offensive play begins or ends. Offensive and defensive volleyball blend together, feeding off one another.

When playing what is apparently offensive volleyball —that is, the ball is being passed and set under control— the team in possession will be preparing to defend their opponent's response to the ball going over the net. Good defense is predicated on first controlling the ball and moving players into position to make offensive play possible. For beginning volleyball players, it is necessary to separate offensive and defensive skills, for purpose of instruction. As players become more experienced and familiar with the transition game, the separation between offense and defense will become less apparent and less important. The game will be played in a rapid, free-flowing manner, blending into an overall system of play.

RECEIVING SERVICE

No system of tactical volleyball play can be successful without skilled, controlled receiving of service. The player who can consistently place the serve into vulnerable areas on the opponent's side of the court or who can serve the ball with great power, spin, or float, is very much on the offensive. Clearly, receiving service starts as a defensive function.

Yet, receiving service must be included in offensive strategy because the ball must first be handled cleanly, under good control, and result in a well-directed, usable pass, thus putting the receiving team onto offense. Once again, the rapid transition from defense in this case to offense, vividly shows the relationship between the two functions. Therefore, it is obvious that receiving service should receive high priority because the flow of attacking volleyball comes from it.

In designing coverage for receiving service, the following factors should go into the basic planning. The majority of serves are directed to the middle third of the court, specifically the area midway between the net and the backcourt end line. Because the ball must clear the net, the front third of the court is less vulnerable to a served ball. Most players serving will want to put the ball deep into the rear third of the court, in the corners, if possible. Experienced, practiced servers can do this. Inexperienced or poor servers will, in the main, just be trying to put the ball into play in front of the backcourt line, but beyond the reach of the spikers at the net and, consequently, serve the ball into the middle third of the court.

The receiving formation or alignment then, should be one that provides good coverage by positioning players in the middle third area of the court. This receiving alignment sets up prescribed zones, with each player responsible for his or her particular zone. The alignment is such that should the server serve short—nearer the net, or deep, nearer the back end line—each player will be able to adjust and cover the zone in front or to the rear of his starting position.

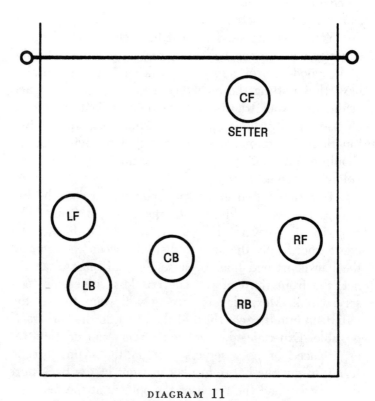

DIAGRAM 11

Basic Alignment for Receiving Serve. The setter or center front (CF) player is positioned near the net, deliberately out of the direct receiving alignment.

Diagram 11 shows the basic alignment for receiving service. The setter or center front court player is positioned near the net, deliberately out of the direct receiving alignment. The front court setter is kept out of the receiving alignment so that he or she will have the freedom to move to setting position to play the set well, unencumbered by having to deal with playing the ball as it comes over the net.

It is best to position the setter to the right of midcourt so that any of the receiving players can pass the ball in front of the setter. In this way, any pass coming up to the net can be played in front of the setter, with the setter having time to get into position to set the ball well.

The server must serve from the right rear third of the court. It becomes apparent then, that the right front court on the receiving team's side of the net, is not particularly vulnerable to a service. Therefore, the receiving alignment should have all five receivers turned to face the player serving with the receiving formation slightly overbalanced to the left.

It is important at this point, especially with beginning players, that each player in the receiving formation should understand his specific zone assignment for the position he is in. Naturally, rotation makes it positively necessary for each player to understand the one assignment for every position on the floor. Assignments are based on two factors. First, the rules of volleyball state that it is illegal to overlap positions when receiving service. In the starting or official receiving position, it is illegal to overlap with the teammate directly in front or in back or on either side until one player touches or plays the ball. Second, assignment of positions is based on ease of getting to the ball to provide the passer with optimum passing accuracy.

With these two points in mind and by using the alignment shown in Diagram 12, receiving responsibilities are as follows.

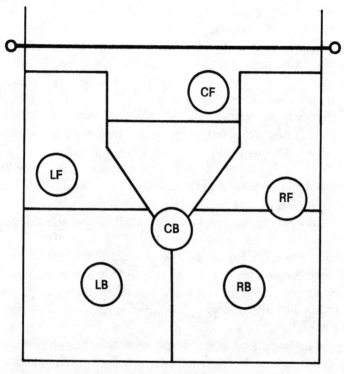

DIAGRAM 12

Zone Coverage Assignments for Receiving Serve. The right and left backcourt players (RB and LB) are responsible for playing any balls that are above waist height on the front line players. The left backcourt player is also responsible for receiving and playing any ball behind the left front court player (LF), as well as any ball passing over the left side to the center backcourt (CB) player. The right backcourt player is responsible for any ball coming over the right side of the center backcourt player, as well as for any ball out of reach of the right front court (RF) player.

The right and left backcourt players are responsible for playing any balls that are above waist height on the front line players. By employing this zonal responsibility, back line players will be able to use the accurate forearm pass to pass the ball forward to the setter. The left backcourt player is also responsible for receiving and playing any ball behind the left front court player, as well as any ball passing over the left side to the center backcourt player.

The right backcourt player is responsible for any ball coming over the right side of the center backcourt player, as well as for any ball out of reach of the right front court player.

In all cases, both the left and right backcourt players should back each other up by going behind the player playing the ball, should the pass go awry. This basic back-up or covering maneuver provides a realistic method for keeping the ball in play in the case of a mishit, errant pass.

The remaining three players, the center back and right and left front court players, are responsible for playing any ball served in front of them, below waist level. This gives them the opportunity to use the forearm pass. These three players are also responsible for any ball served to the right or left of their starting position.

With all players knowing the rules as well as their zone coverage responsibilities for receiving service, handling the opponent's serves will be that much easier. Proper alignment and proper zone assignment will allow players to apply the right kind of forearm pass to the situation. Confusion and hesitation, both fatal to good play and caused by indecision, will be removed. Once proper contact is made with the ball, each player moves to his position according to the type or style of play the team employs.

BASIC OFFENSE

A volleyball team's offense or style of play must be built on the fundamental skill levels of each player, individual capability of each player, individual strengths and weaknesses, individual quickness, and general overall understanding and grasp of team play. While it may seem that the use of the word "individual" is redundant, it must be remembered that a team is made up of individuals, each bringing his or her particular abilities to the team, with each willing to shoulder responsibility for the assignment. To attempt the implementation of a complex style of play for beginning or inexperienced players is a sure invitation to poor play, frustration, discouragement, and many, many defeats.

Rather, offensive tactics should be approached in a positive manner, with the tactics employed based on harnessing the greatest amount of skill and ability brought by each player to the overall team effort. Simplicity in tactical design, when coupled with solid mastery of fundamental skills, will produce competitive, rewarding, and enjoyable team play.

Naturally, as mastery of fundamentals grows and consistent passing, setting, and spiking develop, nuances can be introduced into the overall team strategy with positive results. But, it is essential to begin with a basic system of play to give some order and rationale to the team's play. Later on, as players' experience and team coordination develop, the basic, solid, and more simple systems will serve as the point of departure to more sophisticated styles of team play.

THE 4–2 OFFENSE

It is reasonable to expect that as a team practices, sharpens individual skills, and works on drills, individual players' special skills and talents will emerge, showing whether their particular value to the team will be as a spiker or as a setter. In every sport there are those who best serve as scorers and those whose contribution takes the form of passing and setting. Both are necessary to team play.

With beginning players, where inexperience and less than total mastery of skills is evident, the best system of play from which to build is the 4–2. The reason for this is that the very purpose of the 4–2 is to provide a balance in the distribution of responsibility and play of each player. The name 4–2 reflects having four spikers and two setters on the court, with two spikers and one setter in the front court at all times.

The starting alignment begins with two spikers at the net, one at each corner near the sidelines and the setter in the middle of the court at the net. Of the three backcourt players, two will be spikers with the third being the second setter. (See Diagram 13.)

Starting positions should be taken so that the required rotation will always have one setter at the net. To accomplish this, every third player must be a setter.

At the start of the game, the setter in the front row, at the net, is positioned in the middle of the court between the left and right front court spikers.

The second setter, in the back row, lines up between the left and right backcourt spikers. In this manner, team rotation will always provide one setter for setting duty in the front row, with the other setter in the back row.

The objective of the 4–2 system is to get the one setter in each row into a central distributing point at all times. Obviously, setters have been selected for these

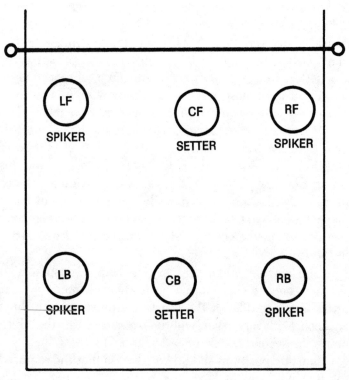

DIAGRAM 13

The 4–2 Offense Starting Alignment. Two spikers are at the net, one at each corner near the sidelines, with the front court setter in the middle. The second setter is in the back row between the left and right backcourt spikers. The 4–2 offense has a setter in each row at all times.

key positions because of their quickness, setting ability, and tactical understanding of the game. In order to take advantage of these talents, setters must be given patterns of play to follow in order that they can easily get into the flow of play and do their job well.

Once rotation begins and players move away from their starting positions, variations of tactics are employed to regain central setter positioning as well as to put the spikers back into the four corners of the court.

The variation most often used is called switching and has as its main purpose, as you would expect, getting the setter at the net to the middle of the court, regardless of the fact that the rotation process has placed the setter in left or right front court positions.

When one of the setters is at the middle of the net at the start of play, there is no need for switching. When a spiker rotates into the center position, the switching situation is on. The setter in the front row changes position (switches) with the spiker, in order to return to the central setting distribution center. (See Diagram 14.)

All players involved in the switch must observe the rule on overlapping positions and so cannot make the switch until the ball is contacted.

A simple example of this play would be as follows. A setter, after rotation, is positioned at either corner of the net. As the serve is made, the setter moves toward the middle of the court while the spiker in the middle moves to the corner of the court vacated by the setter. The setter is now in position to set the ball to either spiker. (See Diagram 15.)

The 4–2 system of play, when combined with practice and smooth switching, allows beginning players the opportunity to employ some deceptive variations to the pass-set-spike pattern and tempo. By getting setters into the central middle court position, forward and back setting can easily be added to play. The technique re-

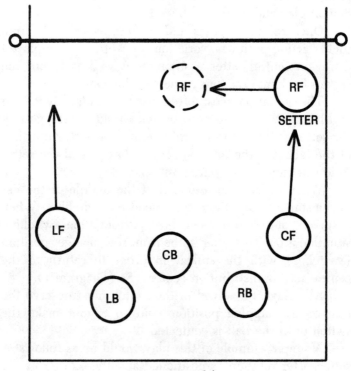

DIAGRAM 14

Switching Variation on the 4–2 Offense. When a spiker rotates into the center position, the setter in the front row to the spiker's right and the spiker switch positions in order to return the setter to the central position.

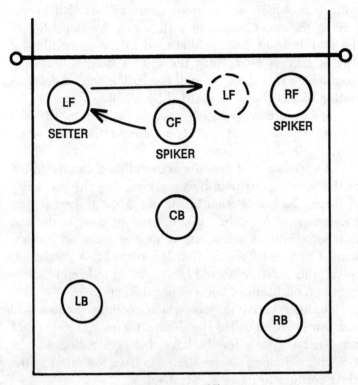

DIAGRAM 15

Switching Variation on the 4–2 Offense. When the setter is in the left front corner of the court with two spikers to his right, as the serve is made the setter moves toward the middle of the court and the spiker in the middle moves to the left front corner.

quired in forward and back setting can also be added. At this time, we are actually employing the skill to disguise the play. In this way, blockers are kept off balance, never quite sure which of the front court spikers will be receiving the set. Competent setters can, by switching to the middle front line position, add to the probability of spiking success by keeping the spikers from anticipating from which side the spike will come. The forced delay in setting blocks is often rewarded by winning spikes.

Some further variation may be added to the 4–2 system of play as players become more skilled and when players blend more smoothly in an overall team effort.

A variation that is easily accomplished can be added to the team's game plan by simply varying the proximity of the set ball in relation to the net. Most spikers prefer, and are more successful, spiking balls set close to the net. But, some spikers are adept at spiking balls set deeper, some 4 to 6 feet from the net. If a team has a good deep spiker, this variation should be employed to keep blockers guessing, off balance, and out of position.

Another variation, one which requires greater skill and teamwork, is called the short set game. The short set game is tailormade for the basic 4–2 system because the 4–2 with switching always strives to have the setter in the ideal position to make an ideal set.

The short set is used to set the ball to a spiker already in the air and poised to spike. The normal set-spike sequence has the setter putting the ball in the air as the spiker approaches the ball.

In the short spike play, the setter, by using a prearranged signal, must set the ball in the air in a one, two spike rhythm. The set is placed to the spiking hand of the spiker while the spiker is in the air. The burden is on the setter to pass the ball in time and with accuracy to the spiking hand. It is this rapid, boom-boom, sequence that gives the short set play its name. While the short set game is difficult, it should be practiced as skills and team play grow.

While the 4–2 system has room for variations, more complex options and tactics are limited by the system itself. However, the 4–2 system's function is to provide the basic framework for developing individual skills and relating those skills to other players' skills, which results in a team approach to the sport. But most important, the 4–2 provides the foundation from which, when players are ready, to build more complex systems of play. As players develop and gain experience, the 4–2 itself will present players with opportunities for expansion as new possibilities emerge from solid fundamental play.

SERVING STRATEGY

The most obvious, important, and the easiest to control factor in terms of maintaining offensive pressure on your opponent is a controlled, well-directed, and well-placed serve. Because the player serving is in control of the situation, from initiation of the serve to the follow-through, there is really no excuse for poor serving. And because everyone must serve at some time in the course of a match, all players must strive for excellence in this vital, offensive skill.

If a server can put the ball into an open area of the court without an opponent playing it, the result is an ace, an immediate score. That is the first and ideal objective of the serve.

The second objective of the serve, and one that is naturally more common to the game, is to serve in such a manner as to force passing errors in the receiving team. Obviously, enforced passing errors result in cutting down the opponent's ability to mount a counterattack.

To intelligently address both objectives of the serve, and by keeping in mind the service variations discussed in the chapter on serving, it remains to examine the areas of the court most vulnerable to good serving.

The sidelines, especially the deeper third of the court, are extremely vulnerable. They are even more vulnerable when a floater or spin serve is used. Float or spin action on a ball served deep toward either sideline has the tendency to force receivers to play the ball toward the sidelines into the out-of-bounds area. This, coupled with the float or spin action on the ball, giving it erratic flight patterns, makes the receiver hard put to make the desired pass to the setter cleanly.

What usually occurs, especially with less experienced players, is that the pass will be played toward the sidelines where no teammate will be able to assist. Any second pass made from the out-of-bounds areas, even if playable, will generally be a poor, inaccurate pass, executed only with the hope of keeping the ball in play. It will not be a controlled pass to a setter. Obviously, this kind of serve disrupts the intentions of your opponent.

Another area of vulnerability is the deep center backcourt area. If you refer back to Diagram 12 on zone coverage when receiving service, you will see that the left and right backcourt players must coordinate their zones to play the serve. Therefore, a floating or spin action serve that is deeply hit into the areas between these two deep players can cause enough indecision and hesitation as to which back should play the ball, resulting in poor handling of the ball.

Indecision and the resultant hesitation can also be caused by placing the served ball between the coverage zone areas of the left front and center backcourt players as well as between the right front and center backcourt players. Short serves take more practice and skill since the ball must first clear the net and then drop just beyond

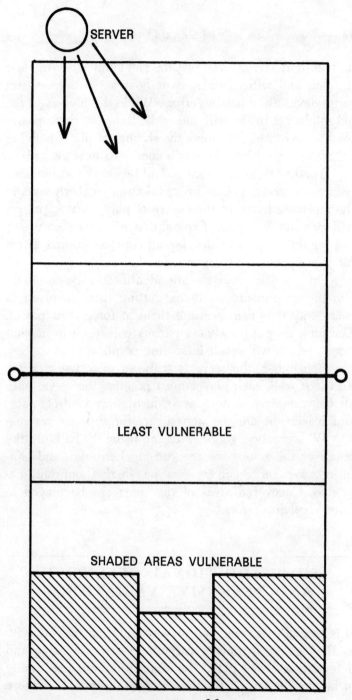

DIAGRAM 16

Areas Vulnerable to the Serve.

it. The short serve, given just the right trajectory to clear the net, and with some spin or float action added, can cause devastating passing errors. While the players at the net might get to the ball and make the pass, these passes tend to be forced and break the rhythm of play by giving the setter something less than a good pass to work with.

Another technique that should be employed by alert, consistent servers is based on exploiting weaker passes in the receiving team. In the course of play, weaker passers will become apparent. Exploitation of a weaker player is a legitimate part of developing court sense and a feel for your opponent's weaknesses and strengths.

Once weaker passers are identified, servers should aim to put pressure on them, getting them involved in every way they can, pressing them to force their passes. The pressure put on weaker passers will result in passing errors, which will result in scoring points.

Remember, the serve is truly an offensive weapon. To use it well, each player must practice the serve, with all its variations, every day. Consistency, control, pace, and placement are the ingredients for superior serving.

With practice, good serves can place the ball into the seams of the zone coverage causing hesitation and confusion. Weaker receivers can be singled out and exploited. Uncovered areas of the court can be played to force receiving errors.

SOME ADDITIONAL OFFENSIVE AND DEFENSIVE VARIATIONS

It is normal that volleyball players and their coaches will, as they gain experience, vary their basic offensive and defensive styles of play. The acquisition and fine tuning of basic skills sets off the natural desire to put these more polished skills into play situations. Coaches and players should extend their curiosity and experiment with the following variations on our basic theme. However, it must always be understood that fundamental skills must be carried out consistently and on a high level in order to be able to accomplish more advanced tactics.

As in football, basketball, and soccer, a single offensive system of play ·in volleyball is not enough. Opponents, also familiar with the basic 4–2 offense, can plan for all its basic variations. They practice against it on a daily basis and, therefore, are alert to virtually every conceivable tactical maneuver that can be dealt from the simpler offensive strategy.

To counter this in all sports, coaches strive to develop variations on the basic theme, that are predicated on the utilization of consistent, well-executed skills, but applied in a wider variety of styles. In most sports, this is termed a multiple offense. While each sport has a different framework from which to base its multiple offense, all have in common expanded roles for specific players, which are then disguised and made to happen in different ways, while appearing to be part of the basic plan.

Volleyball's basic multiple offensive is designed to get more firepower into the attack by using all three players at the net as spikers. The appearance of the lineup is still 4–2, three players in the front court and three in the rear. However, rather than the midcourt front player being a setter, the multiple offense calls for the three front court players to be spikers. All that is left is to design a plan that gets a setter into the right front court area in order to properly utilize the three spikers at the net.

Once again, this style of play is predicated on being able to carry out consistently the fundamental skills, team play, and switching plays that give the basic 4–2 its variations. All that follows is based on and can only be carried out if those skills have been mastered.

MULTIPLE OFFENSIVE VOLLEYBALL

The basic theory of the multiple offensive is to use all three front court players at the net as spikers. The setter then, by design and necessity, must come from one of the three remaining backcourt players. The plan is to get a backcourt player into the right front court area, about 10 to 12 feet from the right sideline.

In this lineup, the setter will have two on-hand spikers to the front to set to and one off-hand spiker at his rear to back set to. Obviously, we have now created a multiple offense in that we now have three spikers available, many more alternatives for a talented and intelligent setter, and many more directions to attack from. There are many ways to achieve the objective of the three-spiker front line. A look at two basic avenues for a team multiple offense follows. These systems are readily applicable to the tactical plans of teams having reached a fairly consistent level of good play. Beyond these approaches are numerous, more sophisticated methods of achieving the variations necessary for high levels of competition.

The two systems are the 5–1 and the 6–2 systems of offense. Both have as their objective three players in spiking position at the net at all times. They vary in how they approach getting setters into the game and the manner in which they achieve that purpose.

THE 5–1 OFFENSE

The 5–1 offense derives its name from its objective of having five spikers on the court at one time. The one in this case refers to the one setter. The plan is to get the one

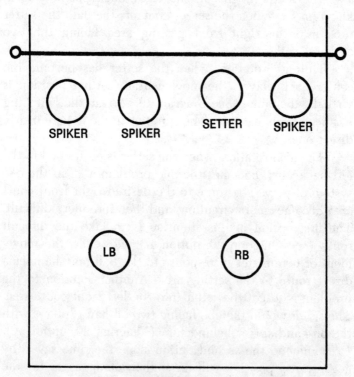

DIAGRAM 17

Multiple Offensive. The object is to have three front court players as spikers, with one of the three remaining backcourt players as the setter. The setter positions himself in the right front court about 10 to 12 feet from the right sideline.

setter into the right front court, after the server contacts the ball, in position to set to any of the three spikers.

The setter begins in the right back position as in Diagram 18. When the server contacts the ball, the setter runs into the right front passing area facing the two on-hand spikers.

Through rotation, when the setter has become the center back player, the movement to setting position is virtually the same. (See Diagram 19.) So far, the switching has been fairly easy since both routes to the net are nearly direct ones.

The next rotation, when the setter is positioned in the left backcourt, becomes the one problem area in the 5–1 system of play. The route to the desired right front court area becomes more circuitous and therefore more difficult. The first option in this situation is to take the difficult route (see Diagram 20, option B). However, the movement of teammates in response to the ball may hamper a direct route to the setting area. Another solution to the problem is to get the setter into the left front court area. The setter would then be facing two off-hand spikers with the on-hand spiker behind him (Diagram 20, option A). I recommend the second option since the time saved by getting into position will more than compensate for the more familiar setting spot. The anxiety and rush in getting to the familiar spot can be more upsetting to play than the every now and then change in basic setting position.

When the setter rotates into the front row, the offense takes on all the basic trappings of the 4–2 system of play. Regardless of rotation along the front line, the setter switches into the center front court setting position with the third spiker drawn from the back line. The basic 4–2 goes on until the setter rotates into the right backcourt position, at which point the procedure starts over again.

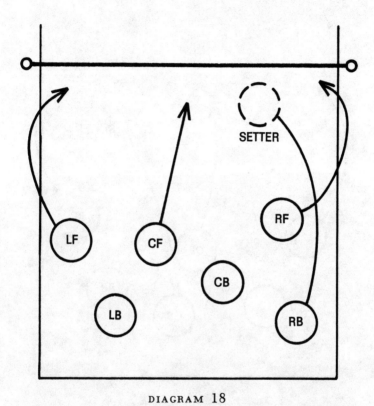

SETTER

DIAGRAM 18

The 5–1 Offense. The object of this offense is to have five spikers and one setter on the court at one time. The plan is to get the one setter into the right front court in position to set to any of three spikers. After the serve, the righ backcourt player moves to the right front court. The left front, center front, and right front players move to the net on both sides of the setter to serve as spikers.

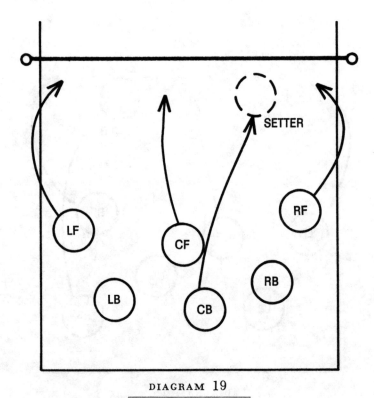

DIAGRAM 19

*The 5–1 Offense. When through rotation the setter becomes
the center backcourt player, the movement to the net is almost
the same as shown in Diagram 18.*

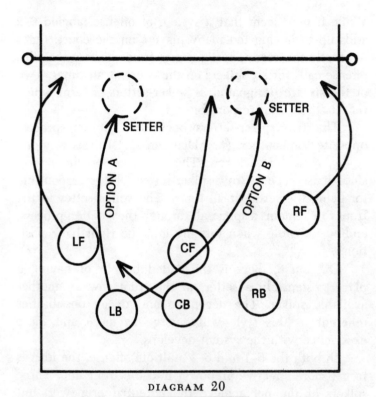

DIAGRAM 20

The 5-1 Offense. When the setter is positioned in the left backcourt, his route to the desired front court area becomes more circuitous and, therefore, more difficult. Option B shows this difficult route, while Option A, a more direct route to the net, puts him in the left front court area. Even though the setter in a left court position will be facing two off-hand spikers with the on-hand spiker behind him, the time saved by getting into position will more than compensate for the more familiar right front court setting spot.

THE 6–2 OFFENSE

While it may seem that a system of offense labeled 6–2 adds up to having too many players on the court, that's not really the case. The six comes from the fact that this offense calls for six spikers on the court at all times. Two of the six are designated as spiker-setters, a term which reflects their dual responsibilities.

The two spiker-setters begin the rotation process opposite one another. (See Diagram 21.) In this way one is always in the back row. This is the key to the system since it is the back row spiker-setter who is responsible for being the setter at all times. The spiker-setter in the front row remains a spiker all through the rotation process, ending that role when rotating into the right back position.

Of course, there is the added benefit of having a player, ostensibly a setter, in the front row as another available spiker. The deception and decoy possibilities inherent in this style will emerge as more and more experience with the system develops.

In both the 5–1 and 6–2 multiple offense, the idea is to get more effective firepower into the front line. Three spikers at the net achieve the potential firepower, but there are variations now possible to enhance the realization of this spiking potential. Until now, we have been looking at basic, regular setting patterns. The setter would get in position and set forward or back, relying on the placement of the set to keep the blockers off balance. But by having three legitimate spikers in the front line presents variations in setting patterns that are sure to confine the blockers on the other side of the net.

Think about the front and back set variation and what is now possible with two on-hand spikers in front.

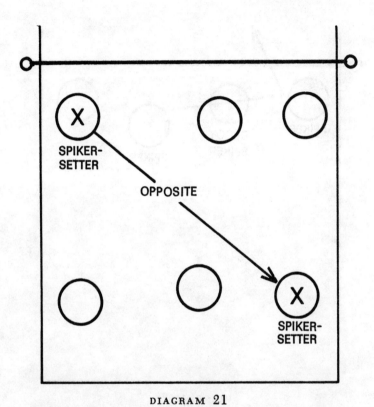

DIAGRAM 21

The 6–2 Offense. This offense calls for six spikers on the court at all times, with two spikers designated as spiker-setters. The two spiker-setters begin rotation opposite each other so that there is always a back-row spiker-setter. The back row spiker-setter is responsible for being the setter at all times, while the front row spiker-setter remains a spiker.

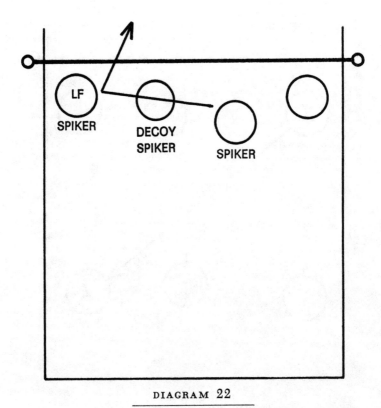

DIAGRAM 22

The Decoy Spiker. With two on-hand spikers in front, opponents can be deceived by having the near spiker jump as if going for the spike but lets it pass to be taken by the second farthest spiker.

The following are some options that will provide deception to the attack.

1. A set to the far front spiker, with the nearer front spiker faking a go at the ball. The near spiker jumps as if going for the spike but lets the ball pass to be taken by the second farthest spiker. (See Diagram 22.)

2. The short set game, in which the spiker is in the air, is excellent for use in the multiple offense. There are two ways to play the short set game in this situation. One way is to set the ball high, about 2 feet above the net. The other way is to set the ball lower, about a foot above net height. In both sets the center front court spiker has made his approach and takeoff and is in the air before the set is made. His spiking arm is cocked and ready to go. Therefore, it becomes the setter's job, should he elect to use this spiker, to put the ball right onto the spiker's hand. Another way to play the short set situation is, with the spiker already launched and poised to strike, the setter has the opportunities of giving the spiker the set or bypassing the spiker in the air and setting the ball to either of the other spikers.

The approach and jump of the center spiker is such a real possibility that when the ball is dealt to another spiker, the defense is out of position and must really scramble for blocking position at the real point of attack.

The timing and accuracy needed to execute these variations are great and will only be achieved after hours of intensive practice. But, this is what development of skills and team play is all about. With practice and hard work, these more advanced skills can be performed.

Training and Conditioning for Volleyball

One of the many reasons volleyball has so much appeal to players and spectators is its consistent action and the varied movements on the part of the players. The rapid transition from offense to defense, the short runs to the ball, the dives, the rolls, the spikes, and the blocks all contribute to making intense physical demands on the players and provide great entertainment for spectators.

As in all team sports, three basic factors must be attained in order to achieve success in volleyball: (1) the acquisition, refinement, and ultimately skillful execution of individual skills; (2) the development of a system of play (tactics) commensurate with the skill levels and capabilities of the players; and (3) the physical fitness necessary to meet the physical demands of the game.

Of the three basic factors, the easiest to attain in a relatively short amount of time is fitness. Fitness is *the* prerequisite for acquiring volleyball skills, since fitness is needed for sustained practice of individual skills. And, certainly, fitness is crucial for sustained participation in a skilled, safe manner in actual volleyball matches.

Modern volleyball coaching theory is built around the ability of individual players to carry out assignments as part of the tactical scheme over the course of an entire game. Regardless of designated position and mindful of the positional changes by rotation, players are required, and indeed forced, to participate fully in the team's total attacking and defensive strategy.

It is obvious that in order to achieve overall team objectives, each player must contribute his or her individual skills to the team effort. To accomplish individual and team objectives, each player must be brought to a high level of physical fitness. This can be achieved only through participation in a carefully planned training and conditioning program that is based on the recognition of the player's physical needs as determined by the demands of volleyball.

To intelligently design a training and conditioning program for volleyball, teachers, coaches, and players must begin with an analysis and inventory of the physical demands made on each player in the course of competition. By delineating the demand components, fitness needs and desired objectives will clearly emerge. With fitness needs understood, the design and implementation of specific training activities can be achieved on a sound, rational, and productive basis.

One more word before we analyze the physical demands made on volleyball players. It has been my experience in teaching and coaching volleyball, tennis, and soccer on all levels, from junior high school on up through high level intercollegiate competition, that by allowing the players to share in the analysis of volleyball's physical demands and by encouraging them to be active partners in the setting of fitness objectives and training activities, players approach training in a more highly motivated way. Motivated players who understand why they are working hard will achieve higher levels of training fitness because they are mentally stimulated to participate in training activities they helped design.

The following is a delineation of physical demands made on volleyball players in the course of a match:

1. Volleyball is basically a game of quick movement. Running consists of rapid bursts of speed over short duration and short distances in pursuit of gaining a position from which to play the ball.
2. Volleyball players must be able to perform quick changes of direction, accelerate, and stop quickly; accelerate and jump vertically from a standing or moving start; accelerate, dive, or roll; move quickly sideways and even backward; and be able to recover quickly from any of the foregoing moves to be in position to play the ball again.
3. While performing any of these movements, the player is expected to be able to pass, set, or spike the ball while on the move, using the legs, trunk, arms, and hands to get to and control the ball.

As we review this inventory of volleyball demands, it becomes apparent that the crucial areas of fitness for volleyball are flexibility, endurance, and strength.

A word of caution at this point. Many coaches attempt to link skill training with conditioning activities. This is done in an attempt to save time by trying to reach skill goals and fitness goals at the same time. It has been my experience, particularly with beginning players, that for the most part it is far better to separate skill training from conditioning work. Developing fitness demands all-out, intensive hard work, whereas skill development, by its very nature, is performed at a much lower work rate. If the objective of the particular activity is to control the ball, the physical work rate is cut because the player cannot control the ball while working and moving with full physical effort.

Conversely, when practicing individual ball control skills, the emphasis is placed on the correct, controlled acquisition and execution of the skill. While in the learning process, the application of intensive physical work will take away from the player's development of coordination, thereby negating the process.

BUILDING CARDIOVASCULAR AND MUSCULAR ENDURANCE

Endurance may be defined as the ability to take part in vigorous physical activity over an extended period of time. For our purposes, strength may be defined as the force with which the muscles contract. Building strength and muscular endurance are related, as will become clearer later on in this chapter.

Volleyball specifically demands repeated short bursts of intensive activity interspersed with longer periods of low to moderate activity. The periods of low or moderate activity provide the player with the time needed to recover from the frequent periods of intensive involvement.

Two kinds of endurance must be achieved for total fitness. The first is cardiovascular endurance, which involves the circulatory and respiratory systems and their function in sustaining total physical activity over long periods of time. The second is muscular endurance, which may be defined as the ability of specific muscle groups to perform their functions repeatedly over extended periods of time. The methods used to build muscular endurance are also employed in building muscular strength. Many of the principles of conditioning are common to both.

By looking at the specific nature of the two kinds of endurance, we will be able to understand better the rationale for training that must go into preparing players for the physical demands of volleyball.

Cardiovascular Endurance

The endurance needed to sustain general total physical effort for long periods of time is called cardiovascular endurance. A look at the basic physiological nature of the cardiovascular system will make clear how this system affects the player.

Virtually every movement we make, as well as nearly every posture the body can assume, is caused by or supported by muscular contractions. Our muscles are constantly at work and, with their every contraction, from the smallest movement to large-scale running movements, they require fuel to provide their energy. This necessary fuel is oxygen, taken from the air and transported by the blood to the muscles.

As the oxygen is used up by the muscles, it must be replaced in the blood. This function is performed by the respiratory system. The respiratory system involves the inhalation of air and is made up of those organs of the body especially equipped to take oxygen from the air and transfer it to the blood. The organs and body parts involved in this process are the nose and mouth, the lungs, and the passages for air that lead to the lungs.

The circulatory system carries the blood to the various parts of the body where the oxygen is needed and used. The circulatory systems also carries the blood away from the muscles, taking with it the wastes that have accumulated as a result of the muscles using and burning the oxygen. The blood then returns to the lungs, where it exchanges the used air and accumulated wastes for freshly reoxygenated air.

The more strenuous the activity, the greater the need for oxygen to support the increased muscular contractions. At this point, the heart's function becomes even more crucial to the circulatory process. The heart is a muscular pump that pumps the oxygenated air into the blood, via the circulatory system, throughout the body. As the need for oxygen increases, the blood must be pumped faster to keep up with the demands for energy being made by the muscles. The harder the muscles work, the harder the heart must pump to circulate the oxygenated blood and remove the wastes of respiration from the body. The signs of this physiological activity are quite clear. As the muscles work harder, the heart speeds up and breathing becomes more rapid, bringing more air into the lungs, all to keep pace with the body's demands.

The conditioning task, then, in training for cardio-vascular endurance is aimed at giving the player the ability to inhale large amounts of oxygen from the air, exchange it in the lungs to the bloodstream, and circulate the oxygen efficiently through the entire body by way of the circulatory system.

This type of conditioning is based on providing the player with aerobic energy, meaning that the energy supplied to the muscles is formed with air or oxygen. Good overall physical fitness is built on having good aerobic energy formation capacity.

To achieve good aerobic capacity, continuous physical activity must be performed regularly. Jogging, cycling, and swimming are examples of cardiovascular endurance builders. The objective is to raise the heart and pulse rate generally above 140 beats per minute and keep the pace at that level for at least five minutes. The idea is to get the body, in its entirety, functioning beyond normal work levels, thus speeding up all the systems involved in general fitness. This kind of training program can be enjoyed by any healthy person, regardless of age, sex, or athletic ability. The one caution that applies to those beginning a fitness program, as well as to those undergoing intensive sports training programs, is that a proper medical checkup be taken before beginning such a program.

Muscular Endurance

While cardiovascular activity is vital to volleyball training, it is simply not enough to meet volleyball's vigorous demands. Therefore, the second kind of endurance needed for volleyball conditioning is muscular endurance.

Muscular endurance may be defined as the ability of the muscles to repeatedly apply force (strength and power) or to sustain muscular contractions over an extended period of time. Muscular endurance, or the lack of it, is easily measured by simply putting the muscles to work at a specific task or activity and then seeing how long they can stay at it.

In volleyball, muscular endurance is most necessary in the legs to sustain the varied and intense patterns of quick acceleration, quick stops, direction changes, jumps and recovery. Without good muscular endurance, players would soon tire, movement to play the ball would slow down, and the ability of muscles and muscle groups to perform complex skills would soon diminish, resulting in poor play.

Old training techniques, not only in volleyball but in all sports, began with endless laps run around gymnasiums and ball fields. This type of training, seen daily on our streets and in our parks, is the now-popular conditioning program called jogging. This kind of running does accomplish increased cardiovascular endurance by developing good aerobic capacity.

However, volleyball is not played at a jogging pace. Being required to accelerate quickly, in short bursts over short distances repeatedly over the course of a series of volleyball games, demands much more than cardiovascular fitness. If muscular endurance has not been attained, cardiovascular fitness will simply not be enough to carry a volleyball player through prolonged competition.

Coaches and players soon realize that the muscular endurance needed to play volleyball had to come from activities specifically designed to make the muscles stronger and more efficient. It was obvious that low or moderate levels of running would not and could not provide the necessary muscular strength and endurance.

The sprint starts, short bursts of speed in all directions, the vertical jumps to spike or block the ball all demand intensive responses to repeated situations. Muscle groups are called on over and over again to perform short-duration intense activities.

The short duration of the specific intensive activity precludes the demand for oxygen since the action is performed and over with rather quickly. The muscles are energized by the store of energy in them, provided by carbohydrates, most notably glycogen. This kind of energy formation is called anaerobic, meaning without air or oxygen.

For a further example of how this energy is used, let us look at a 60-yard-dash sprinter. The sprinter completes the race so quickly that it is unnecessary to breathe at all during the event. Nearly all the energy needed to complete the short dash is stored energy. The cardiovascular endurance factor will come into play, as we shall see later, in the recovery period.

The energy stored in the muscles won't last for more than about two minutes under normal conditions. Muscular endurance training is aimed at conditioning the muscles to tolerate the conversion process of energy into muscular action and to handle the wastes of that conversion more efficiently. The muscles in turn become stronger and more efficient in response to intense demand. The more efficient

the muscles become in working under anaerobic conditions, the greater their tolerance will become for intensive work.

With these basics in mind, it becomes obvious that
muscular strength and endurance and cardiovascular endurance provide the player with the capability for performing repeated, intense, vigorous activities. Cardiovascular endurance provides the overall fitness framework
that allows efficient recovery to be made between heavy
work demands.

PRINCIPLES OF TRAINING

The human body is extremely adaptable in its ability to
accommodate itself to the physical demands put upon it.
Progressive adaptation to the specific demands of a physical activity will result in the increased ability to perform
that specific physical activity. It must be stressed that the
adaptation to or improvement in a specific activity will
only increase the ability to meet that demand generally,
not any other. This means, referring again to our earlier
example, that if players jog to build cardiovascular fitness,
then cardiovascular fitness is what will result. They will
not achieve muscular endurance or strength of the level
needed to sustain repeated sprinting. Training specifically
designed to sustain repeated sprints must involve repeated sprinting.

Therefore, because the body's tendency is to adapt
specifically to demands, volleyball training must be com-
prehensive and specific enough to provide the physical
ability to meet the demands for strength, endurance, and
flexibility that are made on the player in the course of a
game. The following are the four principles involved in
specific training programs.

Overload

The basic principle involved in achieving specific physical improvement is called the overload principle. The overload principle states that the particular activity being performed, whether designed to improve cardiovascular endurance, muscular endurance, strength, or flexibility, must be such that it exceeds in intensity the demands normally made on the individual. It is obvious that an individual is not going to increase strength, for example, unless greater demand is put on his present strength capacity.

Progression

The principle of progression works in concert with overload. As the individual begins applying overload, improvement will soon begin to be seen. If improvement is to continue, progressively greater demands must be made.

This is how overload and progression can be attained in a volleyball training program. In each specific demand area, overloading and progression remain the two underlying principles.

Cardiovascular endurance training requires overloading the large muscle groups of the body, which creates a demand for more oxygen. That demand is met by overloading specifically the respiratory and circulatory systems, resulting in the conditioning of these two vital systems. Overloading for cardiovascular development can be achieved by increasing the rate of speed of the exercise or the distance covered or by combining the two options. This is precisely what jogging, cycling and long-distance swimming aim at and accomplish.

Muscular endurance training requires the overloading of specific muscle groups. The purpose of the overloading is to strengthen the muscles and build tolerance to the strain of work and the resulting anaerobic metabolism taking place. Overloading for muscular endurance is achieved by increasing the work load on the muscles, increasing the repetitions of the specific activity, decreasing the rest intervals between repetitions, or by a combination of any of the three overload methods.

Overloading in flexibility training is accomplished by slowly increasing the range of motion through which the joint and specific muscle group are progressively stretching.

Regularity

In order to realize improvement in physiological and skill capacities, players must train regularly, and preferably on a daily basis. Even when satisfactory fitness levels have been reached, daily workouts are necessary to stay at high competitive levels.

Maintenance

The maintenance principle refers to the rather obvious fact that once high physical fitness and performance levels are reached, it is far easier to maintain that level than it was to achieve it. This principle has particular implications for the off-season. The player will quickly get out of shape if strenuous, regular activity is not kept up. While the activity may not be volleyball, it should be either a sport or training program that will consistently challenge the player's physical fitness.

CONDITIONING ACTIVITIES

Since muscular and cardiovascular endurance as necessary in order to sustain the practice of individual skills and team tactics, we will begin with and base our conditions on drills specifically aimed at these objectives.

Remember, the acquisition of endurance is the result of hard, intensive training. There is no easy way. The skilled coach is able to make the training demanding and, at the same time, varied enough so that players will remain interested and motivated. With some thought and imagination, what might be boring repetitive drills can be transformed into exciting activites.

We base our endurance work training program on the following factors:

1. The age level of the players involved
2. The physical condition the players are in at the start of training
3. The individual differences the players bring to training (size, temperament, experience)
4. The objective of the drill in terms of its specific relationships to game conditions

With these basic factors in mind, the coach must plan intensive running drills that progressively build to the amount of running a player, in his or her age group, will have to endure in a game. There is no set formula for arriving at maximum distances players will have to run in a game. Rather, this judgment must come from the coaches' experience with each age group to determine objectives.

Our endurance and speed training principles are based on the following:

1. Players should be trained to endure the maximum number of yards of intense running, as determined by the coach, based on age level, through intensive running drills.
2. Sprint distances should range between 20 and 40 yards.
3. Whenever possible, running patterns from actual play should be used. Change of direction, quick stops, hurdling over objects should all be part of varied, demanding running activities.
4. Work toward improvement through progressive adaptation of training sprints. This can be done by increasing the number of sprints while maintaining recovery period time, by decreasing the recovery period, or by a combination of the two.

SPECIFIC ENDURANCE DRILLS

Windsprints

Windsprints are invaluable in preparing players for repeated quick-start, full sprints over short distances and are a good example of a specific drill to meet a specific game demand. The all-out sprint from a near stationary position is required many times during play. Through the proper use of windsprints, muscular endurance can be achieved rather quickly and, at the same time, be made into a challenging, fun activity.

To do windsprints, the players begin at a starting line, sprint on command at top speed for 20 to 40 yards, jog back to the original starting line, and, on command, are off again at top speed.

The interval between windsprints should be used to jog to the next starting line or to perform some calisthenics. Twenty seconds between windsprints should be the length of recovery. Windsprints should be done at the beginning and end of each practice session. An average goal of 300 yards at each windsprint session is a good objective.

Tag games and relay races can disguise windsprints, thus making them more palatable and interesting to players. This kind of pressure windsprint running approximates the competitive game situations.

In the course of a volleyball game, players must make abrupt stops, sharp changes in direction, and bursts of acceleration. This all can be incorporated into windsprint drills by coaching commands, to be responded to while running.

Runs made sideways and backward are also called for in games. There should be ample opportunity to practice these movements. Since they are not as intensive in nature as all-out straight-ahead sprinting, they can be used during the recovery intervals between windsprints.

Interval Running

Interval running may be defined as intermittent intensive running in which a given distance is repeated several times with a recovery period in between each intensive run. The recovery period can be taken in the form of walking, jogging, or practicing ball-control skills.

In my experience, I have found that when sprints are broken up into short, intensive runs, with recovery periods between them, players are able to perform greater work loads. This results in more running and better conditioning.

There are three ways of increasing the intensity of interval training for volleyball.

1. Vary the distances to be run
2. Progressively vary the number of times the distance run is to be repeated
3. Vary the time and activity performed during the recovery period

For example, an interval running drill for volleyball might involve running 6 repetitions of 50 yards, each at full speed with a twenty-second rest interval between each sprint. The rest, in this case, would be an easy jog for the twenty-second interval. After the twenty seconds, the players are off again on the next 50-yard sprint.

By applying the three methods for intensifying interval training, we could progressively increase the work rate demand made on the players. This could be done by increasing the sprint distance to 60 yards, by increasing the number of repetitions of the sprint, or by cutting the recovery time.

It is always important to remember that the actual work load in interval training must be determined by the coach within the physiological levels of his players. The system of interval training is good at any level. Working out the demands to be placed on players requires the coach's understanding of objectives as they relate to the needs, level, and capabilities of the players.

When weather permits, running may be done outdoors on a track or grass field. One of the important aspects of windsprint and interval running is their easy adaptability to the field as well as the gymnasium. By utilizing both indoor and outdoor training facilities, higher interest levels are maintained.

DEVELOPING MUSCULAR STRENGTH
AND FLEXIBILITY

Calisthenics play an important part in the training program because they loosen the muscles, warm up players before vigorous activity, and strengthen the muscles to withstand the rigors of volleyball.

Calisthenics are divided into two parts for volleyball purposes: exercises for stretching and loosening up, and exercises for building stronger, more powerful muscles.

Stretching and Loosening Up

These exercises, familiar to most people, are easy to perform and can even be fun. Formations can be a circle or files, with room between the players to allow for easy and free movement. The following exercises should be varied so that players do not lose interest or get distracted easily. Walking or jogging is recommended between each exercise.

1. Neck Rotations. Feet in the straddle position, hands on hips. Rotate head and neck 20 times to the right, 20 times to the left.
2. Arm and Shoulder Rotations. Feet together, arms extended to sides and parallel to ground, palms facing up. Circle arms slowly forward 20 times, backward 20 times.
3. Trunk Twisting. Feet in straddle position, hands on hips, four-count exercise. Lean far to the right, front, left, back, return to upright position, 20 times.

4. Toe Touch, or Windmill. Feet in straddle position, arms extended to sides and parallel to ground. Touch right hand to left toe, left hand to right toe in rhythm, 30 times.

5. Ground Touch. Same position as Windmill. Touch ground with both hands between legs, moving hands farther toward rear, 4 times. (This will loosen back muscles.)

6. Leg Kicks. While walking, alternately kick each leg high into the air, 10 times for each leg.

7. Leg Raises. While walking, alternately bring each knee straight up to the shoulder, 20 times for each leg.

8. Jumping Jack. From attention, jump to straddle position with arms directly over head and hands coming together in a clap, then return to starting position. Build to 50 jumping jacks per calisthenics drill.

9. Groin Muscle Stretch. Spread legs wide apart and alternately squat over one leg while extending fully the other, 10 times to each side.

10. Bicycle Ride. Lie flat on the floor and slowly raise both legs over the head. As legs come up, roll back onto the shoulders. When legs are overhead, pedal as if on a bike, about 50 pedals. Use the arms to maintain balance.

Strengthening Calisthenics

These exercises are designed to toughen the player to withstand the physical demands of competition. Other exercises may be used, but those given here form the core.

For these calisthenics, the player must lie or sit on the grass or gym floor. He runs in place between each exercise.

The player gets to his feet quickly from whatever ground position he has been in, runs in place, and then returns to the ground quickly for the next exercise.

1. Pushups. Standard pushup position. Weight in up position is on fingertips and toes. Body does not touch ground in down position. Build toward 20 pushups.
2. Situps. Flat on back, hands behind head. On up movement, legs are held rigid on ground and elbows are brought to knees, then return to down position, 20 times.
3. Situp Variation. On up movement, twist body so that right elbow touches left knee, then return to starting position. On next up movement, left elbow touches right knee, 10 times for each side.
4. Rocking Horse. Flat on stomach, hands clasped behind back, legs raised from hip. Rock back and forth on chest and stomach, 10 times.
5. Double Leg Raise. Lie on floor. Lift both legs 6 inches from floor, hold for 6 seconds, return to floor, 10 times.
6. Squats. Caution! Deep knee bends are not recommended because of undue strain to the knee. Use half squat. Squat so that the angle of the knee joint remains at more than 90 degrees. Hold for 6 seconds, come back to upright position, repeat 10 times.

The specific exercises in this chapter should form the core of a basic training program for volleyball. By observing the basic principles of training and by being always cognizant of the varied needs of the group being worked with, an intelligent commonsense program can be built around this basic core.

Injuries:
Care and Prevention

Volleyball, while not a body contact sport, makes great physical demands on its participants. Fortunately, part of the inherent appeal of the game is its ability to make demands on players in direct relation to the skill and capability levels of the participants and to the relative importance attached to the particular game being played.

Participants playing in a more social, relaxed, recreational game, even though the competitive spirit may be present, tend to play within the parameters of their skills, game experience, and, of course, at the level of their physical fitness. While many casual players will overexert themselves and feel soreness for a few days following play, injuries tend to be minor ones, albeit similar to the type of injuries incurred by regular competitive players.

On the other hand, participants who play highly competitive "power" volleyball train hard and get into good physical condition. Players who attain this high level of physical conditioning and are prepared for intensive competition over long periods of time, oddly enough, still suffer injuries similar to untrained players. Perhaps the reason for this is that the competitive player has more exposure to possible injury because of far greater time spent in practice or play. But for whatever reason, volleyball has its own particular set of injuries that occur with greater frequency, and for our purposes these are the injuries we will look at.

Taken by itself, volleyball is a sport that has no factors in it that would make it responsible for causing injuries. Football and boxing are easily identified as sports having certain aspects to their games that directly contribute to injuries. If participants train hard and get into total all-around physical fitness, don't take foolish chances, and play with proper equipment, in suitable attire on safe playing surfaces, injuries should be held to a minimum.

INJURIES AND TREATMENT

Sports-related injuries fall into two separate categories—major or disabling injuries, and minor or nondisabling injuries. Each sport has factors in it that can contribute to both categories, and volleyball is no exception. While it is possible for injuries to occur that are not included in this section, through accident, foolish risk taking, or just stupidity, my experience over the years has shown the following injuries to occur most frequently.

Minor or Disabling Injuries

JAMMED OR SPRAINED FINGERS

Jammed or sprained fingers occur with the greatest frequency to inexperienced and unskilled players. Skilled, experienced players rarely have this kind of injury.

The injury is caused first by lack of hand strength directly attributable to not having strengthened, through practice and conditioning, the muscles of the hand. The second contributing factor is lack of skill, which results in poor technique. Improper positioning of the hands and explosive contact with the ball results in stretching and twisting of the finger joints beyond their normal range of motion.

The overall result of traumatic contact between the ball and the fingers will be either jamming or spraining of the finger joints. In jamming, the finger is pushed down into itself. In a sprain, the finger is twisted beyond its normal range. Both injuries may result in great soreness at the affected joints, swelling, discoloration.

Jammed or sprained fingers are best treated by immediate immersion in cold water, and then continuing the application of cold for the first 36 to 48 hours following the injury. The cold minimizes swelling, internal bleeding, which causes discoloration, and eases the pain.

Local support may be given the sore finger or fingers either with the use of a splint or taping the sore finger to its neighboring finger. Elevating the hand by use of a sling will also help ease the pain by keeping the swelling down.

Heat should not be used until after 48 hours have passed. The player should rest the injured fingers until the soreness has gone.

FLOOR BRUISES

Floor bruises have become more common in volleyball since players have been taught to give their all in making defensive plays. Digging and all-out dives and rolls to make a great play by design bring the player into contact with an unyielding and unforgiving floor.

Floor bruises are usually caused by improper technique when floor contact is made after attempting to make a great scoring play.

Prevention of this injury is only possible through training in the proper techniques of falling, diving, and rolling, taught in the same manner as gymnasts are taught the skill. Mats and sand provide good practice surfaces. In the gym or on other hard surfaces, players should practice while wearing hip, elbow, and knee pads until the technique is perfected.

Treatment of floor bruises varies with the severity of the injury. Most bruises are simply treated with ice packs to stop internal bleeding and help reduce any swelling. Apply ice for the first 24 to 36 hours after which time heat should be substituted, thereby increasing circulation to the bruised area. As pain and swelling begin to leave, light exercise and activity may begin, gradually increasing as the injury heals.

Major or Disabling Injuries

SPRAINED ANKLES

Without a doubt, the major disabling injury in volleyball on all levels is the sprained ankle. Whether players are inexperienced beginners or skilled experienced players, sprained ankles are a common occurrence, disastrous to both groups.

Most sprained ankles result from landing on a team-mate's foot after blocking or spiking. In the heat of play, the player or players, leaving the floor to block or spike, return to land on a teammate's foot, turning the ankle into an unstable position with the body's full weight descending onto it. The result is a severely sprained ankle.

The only ways we have found to avoid this "accidental" injury is to (1) work on building better co-ordinated teamwork so that players have a greater sense of their space on the court, (2) strengthen the entire leg through conditioning programs, and (3) teach players to give at the knee as soon as undue weight is felt on the ankle when it is in poor support position. Better the player fall to the floor than risk great weight on an unsupported ankle.

Immediately following the injury and dependent upon its severity, there will be pain, swelling, tenderness, and discoloration resulting from some internal bleeding.

Sprained ankles should be treated by applying ice as quickly as possible. The injured ankle should be elevated and immobilized and referred as quickly as possible to a physician. The quicker the first aid—ice, immobilization, and elevation—and the quicker medical help is called in for diagnosis and treatment, the greater will be the chance for a speedier recovery.

ELBOW AND SHOULDER INJURIES

Elbow and shoulder injuries are most often connected to improper spiking skills. The shoulder and arm are the recipients of the shock transmitted from the body to the ball in the spiking motion. Great strain is put on the shoulder girdle as the arm moves quickly through its arc. The elbow, locked in position, is hyperflexed at contact with the ball. Both of these spiking components bring great strain to both joints.

Two other factors that contribute greatly to shoulder and elbow injuries are a lack of strength in these joint areas due to poor conditioning or failure to warm up properly.

The most frequent injury to the elbow, regardless of the sport it occurs in, is called tennis elbow. Treat elbow injuries with ice immediately and continue for 24 to 36 hours. Following the cold treatment period, warm soaks should be applied. Rest and warm soaks should continue until pain is gone.

Most volleyball shoulder injuries are of the strain or sprain variety and should be treated as such. Begin treatment with the application of ice, and then the injured shoulder should be immobilized. Immobilization on a first-aid basis is easily accomplished by use of a sling, which takes weight off the shoulder joint.

In shoulder injuries, the best policy to follow is ice, immobilize, and referral as quickly as possible to a physician who can determine the extent of the injury.

The key to preventing these and most other volleyball injuries lies in the progressive, well-planned physical conditioning program used to get players ready for competition. Risk of injury is present in every athletic event and will happen even to the best conditioned athlete.

However, frequency of injury can be limited through thorough training, intelligent play, proper equipment and facilities, and, of course, thorough use of skilled technique.

Glossary

Antenna
A vertical rod attached to the outside edge of the net at each sideline, extending 2½ to 3 feet above the net. A ball hitting either antenna is deemed out of bounds.

Attack block
An attempt to intercept the ball before it passes over the net.

Back set
A set made over the setter's head to the spiker to the rear of the setter.

Block
A defensive maneuver by one or more players in an attempt to intercept the ball over or near the net.

Bump pass
Passing in an underhand manner using the forearms as the contact surface.

Contacted ball
A ball that is touched by or touches any part of a player's clothing.

Crosscourt serve
A serve made to the opponent's right sideline.

Dig
Underhand forearm pass used to play spikes or any ball dropping close to the floor.

Digging
Passing a hard-spiked ball while standing, diving, or rolling for it.

Dink
A variation of the spike, in which the fingertips are used to lift the ball over the spike-anticipating blockers.

Dive
An attempt at recovering a low ball by stretching out in a prone position to get the arms under the ball.

Double block
Two players working in tandem to make the block at the net.

Floater serve
Generally an overhand serve with no spin that travels on an erratic path as it nears the receiver. The ball is hit briskly with no follow-through.

Foul
Illegal play of the ball as defined by game rules.

Line serve
A serve made in a straight line aimed along the opponent's left sideline.

Netting
Making contact with the net while the ball is in play. Netting terminates play, with the offending team losing possession of the ball or loss of the point.

Off-hand side
The side of the court on which the spiker contacts the ball with the predominant hand after it crosses the spiker's body.

Off-speed spike
A ball that quickly and deliberately loses impetus because the striking arm speed has been slowed just prior to impact.

On-hand side
The side of the court on which the spiker contacts the ball with the predominant hand before it crosses the spiker's body.

Out-of-bounds
A ball is out-of-bounds when it touches any surface or object outside the court, touches a net antenna, or touches the net outside the markers on the net sides.

Overhand pass
A pass executed with both hands held at head height with the ball passed in the direction the passer is facing.

Overhand serve
A serve executed with an overhand throwing action.

Roll
Movement to the side that allows a player to get under the ball, make contact with the ball, contact the floor, roll, and recover, without injury.

Scoring
Only the serving team can score a point. One point is awarded for each score.

Seam
The vulnerable areas generally between two serve receivers or two players whose areas of responsibility overlap.

Serving
The act of putting the ball into play by striking it, having it clear the net and land within the boundaries of the opponent's court.

Set
An overhand pass designed to place the ball into position for a teammate to spike.

Setter
The player whose function it is to set the ball to the spiker.

Spike
A ball hit with great force into the opponent's side of the court.

Spiker
The player executing the power spike or variations, such as the off-speed spike or dink.

Spin serve
A serve in which the ball is contacted just below the horizontal midline by the heel of the hand. Wrist snap draws the fingers over the ball to impart spin.

Side out
The exchange of service after the serving team has failed to score a point.

Thrown ball
A judgment decision made by a game official as to whether a ball was contacted cleanly or visibly came to rest at contact. A thrown ball is a foul.

Underhand serve
Basic serving technique for beginning players. Ball is struck with an underhand striking motion with the heel of the hand.

The Rules

The following summary of volleyball rules was prepared from the Rules of the Game as developed by the United States Volleyball Association. Official Rules can be purchased from USVBA Sales, 1750 East Boulder Street, Colorado Springs, Colorado 80909.

Rule 1. Playing Area and Markings

The playing court should be 59 feet by 29 feet 6 inches with a center line drawn across the court beneath the net, dividing the court into two equal playing areas.

The attack line should be drawn parallel to and 9 feet 10 inches from the center line in each playing area. The attack area is limited by the center line and the attack line.

The service area is behind the end line from the right sideline 9 feet 10 inches toward the left sideline.

Rule 2. The Net

The net should be at least 32 feet in length and 39 inches in width.

Net height, measured from the center of the court, should be 7 feet 11⅝ inches for men and 7 feet 4⅛ inches for women. These net heights are used for players age fourteen and older. For the age group eleven and under, the height for girls and boys is 6 feet 1 inch. For the thirteen and under age group, the height for girls is 7 feet 2 1/16 inches and for boys 7 feet 4⅛ inches.

Vertical tape markers should be placed at each end of the net perpendicular to and directly over the sidelines. The markers are considered part of the net.

Net antennas should be placed on the outside edge of the vertical tape markers. Antennas should be 6 feet in length and made of a safe, flexible material.

Net supports should be at least 19½ inches from the sidelines.

Rule 3. The Ball

The volleyball should have a laceless leather or leatherlike cover of twelve or more pieces. It must be between 25 and 27 inches in circumference, of light uniform color, and weigh no less than 9 and no more than 10 ounces.

Rule 4. Rights and Duties of Players
and Team Personnel

All coaches and players should know the rules and abide by them. The coaches, managers, and captains are responsible for proper conduct of their team personnel. The playing captain is the spokesman of the team and the only player who may address the first referee.

Requests for time-out may be made by the head coach and/or by the playing captain when the ball is dead. Each team is allowed two time-outs per game. Each time-out is limited to 30 seconds and players are not allowed to leave the court and may not speak to anyone except to receive advice from a coach who is nearby but not on the court.

Acts subject to sanction include addressing officials concerning their decisions; making profane or vulgar remarks to officials, opponents, or spectators; coaching during the game by any team member; shouting or yelling to distract an opponent who is playing or attempting to play a ball; attempting to influence decisions of officials; and clapping hands at the instant of contact with the ball by a player, particularly during the reception of service.

Offenses committed by coaches, players, and other teammates may result in a warning, penalty, expulsion from the game, or disqualification from the match. A warning (yellow card) is issued for minor unsporting offenses, such as talking to opponents, and a second minor offense may result in a penalty. A penalty (red card) is issued for rude behavior or a second minor offense. It automatically entails loss of service by the offending team, if they are serving, or the awarding of a point to the opponents if they are not serving. A second act warranting a penalty results in the expulsion of the player or team member. Expulsion of a player from the game (red and yellow cards together) comes from offensive conduct (such as obscene gestures) toward officials, spectators, or opponents. A second expulsion during a match disqualifies the player. A player can also be disqualified (red and yellow cards apart) for any attempted or actual physical aggression toward officials, spectators, or opponents. Disqualified persons must leave the area, including the spectator area, of the match.

Rule 5. The Teams

Players' uniforms should consist of a jersey, shorts, and light and pliable shoes with rubber or leather soles and without heels. Jerseys should be marked with numbers on the front and the back.

A team consists of six players plus substitutes, but may not exceed a total of twelve players.

Before the start of a match the head coach or captain of each team should give the scorer a lineup of players who will be starting the game and what positions they will play. A team is allowed six substitutions per game, which may be made when the ball is dead at the request of the playing captain. A player starting a game may be replaced only once and may subsequently enter the game once, but in the original position in the serving order in relation to other teammates. Only the original starter can replace a substitute during the same game.

Rule 6. Team Areas, Duration of Matches, and Interruptions of Play

International matches consist of the best of three out of five games.

The toss of a coin by the two captains determines first serve and team area for the first game. The winner of the toss picks the option. There is a new toss of the coin for first serve and team area for the deciding game of a match. Otherwise, teams change sides after each game. In a deciding match, when one team reaches 8 points, the teams change sides, but serving continues by the player whose turn it is to serve.

Two-minute intervals are allowed between games of a match, except between the fourth and fifth games, where the interval is five minutes.

If a referee notices an injured player or something on the court that could be a hazard, play is stopped. When the game resumes, a playover is called.

Rule 7. Commencement of Play and the Service

The server has 5 seconds after the referee's whistle in which to release or toss the ball for service. When the ball is hit for service, the server must not have any part of his body in contact with the end line, the court, or the floor outside the lines of the service area.

A side-out occurs after one of the following service faults: the ball touches the net or passes under it, the ball touches an antenna and does not pass between the antennas, the ball touches a player of the serving team, or the ball lands outside the limits of the opponent's playing area.

A player serves until a fault is committed by the serving team.

Players rotate one position clockwise after the team receives the ball for service and before the ball is actually served.

Players of the serving team cannot prevent their opponents from watching the server or the ball's trajectory by screening.

Before the ball is contacted for the serve all players must be in the position listed on the scoresheet, with the exception of the server. After contact with the ball is made, players may move from their assigned positions.

Rule 8. Playing the Ball

Each team can make up to three successive contacts of the ball in order to return the ball to the opponent's area.

The ball can be hit with any part of the body on or above the waist.

The ball can contact more than one part of the body as long as the contacts are simultaneous.

The ball must not come visibly to rest in the hands or arms of a player. It must be hit so that it rebounds cleanly or it will be considered as having been held.

When two team players contact the ball simultaneously, it is considered two team contacts and neither of the two players can make the next play on the ball.

A player cannot attack the ball on the opponent's side of the net.

Rule 9. Play at the Net

A ball hitting the net between the antennas, other than a served ball, may be replayed.

If a player contacts the net during play, accidentally or not, he is charged with a fault.

If a player contacts the opponent's area with any part of his body except his feet, it is a fault. However, part of the foot must remain on or above the center line.

Rule 10. Dead Ball

A ball is dead when it touches an antenna or the net outside an antenna; when it does not cross the net completely between the antennas; when it strikes the floor, wall, or any object attached to the wall; when it hits the ceiling or something hanging from the ceiling; when a player commits a fault; when a served ball hits the net or another object.

Rule 11. Team and Player Faults

A double fault occurs when players of both teams simultaneously commit faults, resulting in a playover.

The penalty for a fault by the serving team is a side-out; the penalty for the receiving team is the awarding of a point to the serving team.

The following are team or player faults: when the ball touches the floor, is held, thrown, or pushed, or touches a player below the waist; when a team plays the ball more than 3 times consecutively or when a player touches the ball twice consecutively; when a team is out of position at service; when a player touches the net or antenna, completely crosses the center line into the opponent's area, or attacks the ball above the opponent's playing area; when a backline player in the attack area hits the ball into the opponent's court from above the height of the net; when a ball does not cross the net entirely between the antennas or it lands outside the court or touches an object outside the court; when a ball is played by a player with assistance by a teammate as a means of support; when a player receives a personal penalty or when he reaches under the net and touches the ball or an opponent while the ball is being played by the opposite team; when a team, after havng been warned, receives instructions from the coach, manager, or substitutes; when a game is persistently delayed or an illegal substitution is made; when a team makes a fourth request for a time-out after a warning or if the second time-out extends beyond 30 seconds; when there is a delay in making a substitution after having used the two time-outs; when a player, after being warned, leaves the court during the interruption of play without permission of the first referee during a game; when players stamp their feet or make distracting sounds or gestures toward opponents; and when illegal blocking or service is performed.

Rule 12. Scoring and Results of the Game

When a receiving team commits a fault, the serving team gets a point.

A game is won by the team to first get 15 points with at least a 2-point advantage.

If a team does not have sufficient players to start a game or refuses to start a game after the referee requests play to begin, the team shall lose by default with the score recorded as 15–0.

Rule 13. Decisions and Protests

Referee and other officials' decisions are final.

Disagreement over the interpretation of rules must be brought to the first referee prior to the first service after the play in question.

Rule 14. The First Referee

The first referee is in full control of the match with authority over all players and officials. He also has the power to settle all questions not covered by the rules and can overrule decisions of other officials.

The first referee should be located at one end of the net during play.

Rule 15. The Second Referee

The second referee should be located at the opposite end of the net from the first referee. He assists the first referee in making such calls as violations of the center line, contact with the net by a player, and the ball not crossing the net entirely.

The second referee also is the timekeeper of time-outs and rest periods between games, and he supervises the conduct of coaches and substitutes and substitutions requested by captains or head coaches.

Rule 16. The Scorer

The scorer should be located behind the second referee.

The scorer records the scores as the match progresses, makes sure that the serving order and rotation of players is followed correctly, checks the number of substitutes, and records time-outs.

Rule 17. The Line Judges

If there are two line judges in a match, they should be located diagonally opposite each other in the nonserving corners of the court.

If there are four line judges in a match, they should be located at each corner of the court.

Line judges signal whether balls are in or out, foot fault errors of servers, when the ball touches an antenna or does not pass over the net completely between the antennas.

Special Rules

Coed Play

The rules apply in general with the following exceptions: the positions on the court and the serving order must alternate male-female or vice versa; if the ball is played more than once by a team, one contact must be made by a female player (male players do not have to contact the ball); if only one male player is in the front line at service, one male backcourt player may be forward of the attack line in order to block; and the height of the net should be 7 feet 11⅝ inches.

Reverse Coed Play

The special rules are the same as for Coed Play except read "male" where it says "female," and "female" where it says "male."

Beach Play

The general rules apply with the following exceptions: the net height should be 7 feet 10 inches on hard-packed sand and 7 feet 8½ inches on loose-packed sand; teams switch playing areas during each game after multiples of 5 points have been scored; and ropes are used as boundary lines and the center line.

Doubles Play

The general rules apply for two-player (doubles) teams with these exceptions: each team area should be 25 feet long; there are only two positions (left and right half areas) and no substitutions allowed; service can be made from anywhere behind the end line; and the game is won at 11 points.

Index